BREAKFAST BURRITO ....
    EGGS AND SWEET POTATO PESTO 3
    SMOKED PAPRIKA EGG CASSEROLE 4
    SMOKED HAM AND BABY SPINACH MIX 5
    YOGURT WITH FRUITS 6
    BACON AND CHEESE CRUSTLESS QUICHE 7
    CINNAMON-RAISIN FRENCH TOAST BREAKFAST 8
    BACON CHEESE ROLLS 10
    GRANOLA CRUMBLE 11
    CASSEROLE BREAKFAST 12
    BREAKFAST BREAD 13
    FRUITY QUINOA MORNING 14
    LEEK STIR-FRY 15
    SWEET OATMEAL 16
    TOMATO COUSCOUS 17
    INDIAN GREENS BREAKFAST 18
    BREAKFAST BREAD BOATS 19
    RICOTTA AND SAUSAGE-CRUSTED PIE 20
    SPINACH EGGS MORNING 22
VEGETABLES AND VEGAN 23
    EGGPLANT PARMIGIANA 23
    EGGPLANT IN CHILI SAUCE 24
    HASH BROWN CASSEROLE 26
    GARLIC AND PARMESAN ASPARAGUS 27
    ORIENTAL BROCCOLI 28
    VEGGIE-NOODLE SOUP 29

KETO SOUFFLE 30

ENCHILADA AMARANTH 31

VEGGIE FAJITAS 32

VERITABLE FEAST CURRY 33

CREAMY SCALLOPED POTATOES 35

SOUR CREAM MUNG BEANS 36

COTTAGE PIE 37

RED CABBAGE WITH GARLIC 38

SIMPLE PRESSURE COOKER CHICKPEA HUMMUS....39

SIMPLE HEALTHY BEANS RECIPE 40

POTATOES AU GRATIN 41

LOVEABLE BRUSSELS SPROUTS 42

CLASSIC CAULIFLOWER SPREAD WITH THYME 43

SOUPS AND STEWS 44

PIZZA SOUP 44

BEEFY ONION AND BLUE CHEESE SOUP 45

VELVETY MUSHROOMS AND BROCCOLI SOUP 47

CLAM CHOWDER...47

BEEF BARLEY SOUP...48

ASPARAGUS AND SORREL BISQUE 50

BACON AND POTATO SOUP 51

TUSCAN CANNELLINI BEAN SOUP 52

EASY BEEF AND CABBAGE SOUP 54

CHICKEN AND ZUCCHINI NOODLE SOUP...................................55

SUPER-GREEN SOUP 56

LEEK AND POTATO SOUP 57

RABBIT CABBAGE STEW..58

- WHITE CHICKEN CHILI 59
- GINGERED CHICKEN BROTH 60
- INDIAN CURRIED BROCCOLI SOUP 62
- BEST BEANS-FREE CHILI 63
- BEEF BORSCHT SOUP 64
- CHICKEN AND BEANSPROUTS 65

FISH AND SEAFOOD 66
- SQUID STEW 66
- SHRIMP SCAMPI 68
- CREAMY MUSSEL SOUP 69
- BALSAMIC CATFISH 70
- TILAPIA TOMATO STEW 71
- INSTANT POT MOK PA 72
- SHRIMP DIABLO 74
- LIGHT LOBSTER SOUP 75
- SQUID RINGS WITH SPINACH AND POTATO 76
- CREOLE SHRIMP 78
- HERBED MOROCCAN TILAPIA 79
- CREAMY SHRIMP STEW 80
- BROCCOLI SALMON 81
- SEAFOOD PAELLA 82
- ADOBO SHRIMPS RECIPE 84
- TUNA SALPICAO 85
- KETO SEAFOOD STEW 86
- SEAFOOD JAMBALAYA 88
- BUTTERY SALMON WITH ONIONS AND CARROTS 89

CHICKEN AND POULTRY 90

KUNG PAO CHICKEN	90
SLOW CHICKEN CURRY	91
LEMON SAUCE PULLED CHICKEN	92
GLAZED DUCK BREAST	94
CHICKEN SATAY	95
GARLIC LEMON CHICKEN	96
CREAMY MEXICAN CHICKEN	98
CREAMY GARLIC TUSCAN CHICKEN THIGHS	99
CHICKEN FAJITA	101
ROSEMARY CHICKEN WITH BACON	102
GARAM MASALA CHICKEN	103
GAME DAY BUFFALO WINGS	105
SHREDDED CHICKEN WITH SHIITAKE	106
CHICKEN AND PINEAPPLE	108
WHITE CHICKEN CHILI	109
CORIANDER SHREDDED CHICKEN	110
CHICKEN CHEESE RECIPE	111
CREAM CHEESE CHICKEN	112
CITRUS HERB CHICKEN CHORIZO	113
ITALIAN BUFFALO CHICKEN	115
KNOCK OFF YOUR SOCKS CHICKEN AND SAUSAGE	116
FLAVORED TURKEY WINGS	117
INSTANT POT CHICKEN BIRYANI	118
CHICKEN SAUSAGE AND KALE SOUP	119
TURKEY CAULIFLOWER MEAL	121
SALMON FILLETS AND LEMON SAUCE	122
SPICY TURKEY BREAST	123

- SWEET TURKEY DRUMSTICKS 124
- TURKEY MINESTRONE 125

PORK, BEEF AND LAMB 126
- STEAK AND BEANS 126
- WESTERN SHOULDER RIBS 127
- CHUNKY AND BEANLESS BEEF CHILI 128
- BRAZILIAN BEEF STEW (FEIJOADA 129
- LAMB RIBLETS WITH HERBS 130
- MEATY STUFFED PEPPERS 132
- ITALIAN BEEF SANDWICH FILLING 133
- PULLED PORK WITH BBQ RUB 134
- BEEF PICADILLO 135
- DOUBLE-SMOKED BACON AND LEEKS 137
- BRATWURST STEW 138
- EASY BEEF AND BROCCOLI STIR FRY 140
- ROSEMARY BEEF 141
- EASTERN MEAT LOAF 142
- TOMATO PORK CHOPS 143
- BRAISED PORK LOIN WITH PORT AND DRIED PLUMS 145
- PORK AND CABBAGES 146
- LAMB SHANK WITH BURGUNDY 147
- EASY BEEF CHILI 148
- PULLED PORK 149
- TERIYAKI PORK TENDERLOIN 150
- BEEF CURRY 151
- LAMB STEW 152
- ASIAN BEEF SHORT RIBS 153

- SLOWLY COOKED LAMB SHOULDER KEBAB 154
- BAJA PORK TACOS 156
- JUICY POT ROAST 157
- JAMAICAN JERK PORK 158
- CHEESY MEAT PASTA 159

SNACKS AND APPETIZERS 160
- SPICY SAUSAGE APPETIZER 160
- INCREDIBLE SPINACH DIP 161
- SAUSAGE DIP 162
- SLOW COOKER CHEESE DIP 163
- CAULIFLOWER DIP 164
- TENDER ALMOND SHRIMPS 165
- KIDS FAVORITE PECANS 166
- ARTICHOKE SPREAD 168
- THREE-CHEESE SPAGHETTI SQUASH 169
- SHIITAKE MUSHROOM BITES 170
- BANANA BREAD 171
- SMOKIES 172
- SLOW COOKER MEATBALLS WITH SESAME SEEDS 173
- RADISH LEMON SNACK 175
- TRADITIONAL BRITISH SCOTCH EGGS 176
- BROCCOLI BITES 177
- POOL-PARTY MEATBALLS 178
- SOUTHERN BOILED PEANUTS 179
- SHRIMP BOIL 180

DESSERTS 181
- PARSLEY DIP WITH BLUE CHEESE 181

NUTELLA GRANOLA	183
ROSEMARY FINGERLING POTATOES	184
CHARLOTTE	185
ALMOND STRAWBERRY SQUARES	186
PORK CHEESE ROLLS	188
SPICY SAUSAGE APPETIZER	189
PEANUT CHICKEN STRIPS	190
KETO MOCHA DE CREME	191
ALMOND AND CHOCOLATE CANDY	193
FISH STICKS	194
LEEK DIP	195
BEEF LETTUCE WRAPS	195
ZINGY BOILED PEANUTS	196
CHEESECAKE	198
TENDER ALMOND SHRIMPS	199
CLEAN EATING BLONDIES	200
MINTY GRAPEFRUIT MIX	201
MINI SAUSAGES DELIGHT	202

BREAKFASTS

BREAKFAST BURRITO

Serving: 4

Ingredients:

- 1-pound chicken fillet, chopped
- ½ cup of water
- 1 teaspoon butter
- 1 tablespoon mayonnaise
- ½ avocado, chopped
- 1 tomato, chopped
- 1 teaspoon chili flakes
- 1 teaspoon salt
- 4 keto tortillas
- 1 tablespoon fresh cilantro, chopped

Directions:

- Place chicken, water, butter, and salt in the crockpot.
- Close the lid and cook the ingredients for 8 hours on Low.
- When the chicken is cooked, chill it to the room temperature.
- Meanwhile, spread the tortillas with mayonnaise and sprinkle with chili flakes and fresh cilantro.
- After this, add avocado and tomato.
- Then add cooked chicken fillet.
- Roll the tortillas in the shape of burritos.

Nutrition:

- Calories - 368
- Fat - 19.5
- Carbs - 7.7
- Protein - 39.5

EGGS AND SWEET POTATO PESTO

Serving: 4

Ingredients:

- 4 sweet potatoes, pricked with a fork
- 4 eggs, fried
- 2/3 cup walnuts, soaked for 12 hours and drained
- 1 garlic clove
- 1 and ½ cups basil leaves
- ½ cup olive oil
- Juice from ½ lemon
- A pinch of salt and black pepper

Directions:

- Wrap sweet potatoes in tin foil, add them to your slow cooker, cover and cook on High for 4hours.
- In your food processor, mix walnuts with garlic, basil, oil, salt, pepper and lemon juice and pulse really well.
- Mix sweet potato mash with basil pesto and stir well.
- Divide fried eggs between plates, top each with sweet potato pesto and serve for

- breakfast.
- Enjoy!

Nutrition:

- Calories - 163
- Fat - 5
- Carbs - 13
- Protein - 4

SMOKED PAPRIKA EGG CASSEROLE

Serving: 5

Ingredients:

- 4 oz ham, chopped
- 1 tablespoon dried dill
- 1 tablespoon smoked paprika
- 2 bell peppers, chopped
- 1 tablespoon ricotta cheese
- 1 tablespoon almond flour
- ½ teaspoon cayenne pepper
- 1 teaspoon salt
- 5 eggs, whisked
- ½ cup heavy cream
- 4 oz Cheddar cheese, shredded
- 1 teaspoon olive oil

Directions:

- Brush the crockpot with olive oil from inside and arrange ½ part of ham in it.

- Then mix up together dried dill, smoked paprika, almond flour, cayenne pepper, and salt.
- In the separated bowl, mix up together heavy cream and whisked eggs.
- Place the chopped bell peppers over the ham and add the layer of the remaining ham.
- Then sprinkle the mixture with smoked paprika mixture.
- Add whisked egg liquid and shredded Cheddar cheese.
- Then add ricotta cheese and close the lid.
- Cook the casserole for 8 hours on Low.

Nutrition:

- Calories - 298
- Fat - 22.6
- Carbs - 8
- Protein - 17.6

SMOKED HAM AND BABY SPINACH MIX

Serving: 2

Ingredients:

- 2 tablespoons olive oil
- ¼ cup coconut milk
- 2 eggs, whisked
- 4 ounces cooked smoked ham, chopped
- 1 cup baby spinach
- A pinch of black pepper

Directions:

- Heat up a pan with the oil over medium heat. Add the ham and black pepper, stir, cook for 5 minutes and In a bowl, mix the eggs with the coconut milk, spinach and some more black pepper.
- Whisk well and pour over the ham.
- Stir everything gently in the slow cooker, cover and cook on low for 4 hours.
- Divide between plates and serve for breakfast.

Nutrition:

- Calories - 348
- Fat - 30,5
- Carbs - 4,7
- Protein - 16.1

YOGURT WITH FRUITS

Serving: 10

Ingredients:

- 1 gallon of milk
- ½ cup Greek yogurt
- 2 tablespoons vanilla bean paste
- 2 cups fruit of your own choice
- 1 cup sugar

Directions:

- Pour the milk into the Instant Pot.

- Close the lid and secure the vent.
- Press the Adjust button until the display indicates "boil". This will pasteurize the milk for 45 minutes.
- Once done, remove the inner pot from the Instant Pot and pour the milk into a clean jar. allow the milk to cook for 115 degrees Fahrenheit.
- Clean the inner pot back into the Instant Pot and plug it in.
- Pour in the milk, Greek yogurt, and vanilla bean paste into the Instant Pot and press the Yogurt button. The timer with reading 0: 00 and adjust it to 8 hours.
- Close the lid and allow the yogurt to ferment for 8 hours.
- Once done, place inside clean jars and refrigerate before serving.
- Once ready to serve, add fruits and sugar.

Nutrition:

- Calories - 172
- Carbs - 24.6g
- Protein - 3.8g
- Fat - 2.3g

BACON AND CHEESE CRUSTLESS QUICHE

Serving: 6

Ingredients:

- 6 eggs, lightly beaten

- 1 cup milk
- Salt and pepper to taste
- 2 cups Monterey Jack cheese, grated
- 1 cup bacon, cooked and crumbled

Directions:

- Spray the inner pot of the Instant Pot with cooking spray.
- In a mixing bowl, mix together the eggs, milk, salt, and pepper until well-combined.
- Place the bacon and cheese in the Instant Pot and pour over the egg mixture.
- Close the lid and press the Manual button. Adjust the cooking time to 10 minutes.
- Do natural pressure release.

Nutrition:

- Calories - 396
- Carbs - 5.5g
- Protein - 23.7g
- Fat - 31.3g

CINNAMON-RAISIN FRENCH TOAST BREAKFAST

Serving: 6

Ingredients:

- ½ cup packed light brown sugar
- 7 large eggs
- 16 cinnamon-raisin bread slices, cubed

- 1 cup heavy cream
- 2 ½ cups whole milk
- Non-stick cooking spray
- 2 cups pecans or walnuts (optional

Directions:

- Tightly line your slow cooker with foil and coat with non-stick spray.
- Pour the bread cubes into the prepared slow cooker.
- Whisk together the milk, eggs, cream, and sugar (2 cups of pecan or walnuts, optional).
- Pour the egg mixture over the bread in a slow cooker, and push down the bread a bit so it can soak in the egg.
- Cover and cook on LOW for 4 hours (or HIGH for 2 hours).
- Remove the top from the slow cooker, turn off the heat, and allow cooling for 15 minutes.
- Serve.

Nutrition:

- Calories - 149
- Fat - 7 g
- Carbs - 16 g
- Protein - 5 g

BACON CHEESE ROLLS

Serving: 3

Ingredients:

- 6 large eggs
- ½ cup cheddar cheese
- 6 bacon slices
- 2 tbsp green onions, finely chopped
- Spices: 1 tsp salt
- ½ tsp black pepper, ground
- ½ tsp dried oregano, ground

Directions:

- In a large mixing bowl, combine eggs, cheddar cheese, green onions, salt, pepper, and oregano.
- Whisk until well combined and foamy. Set aside.
- Grease 6 silicone muffin molds with some cooking spray. Line the walls of each cup with bacon and pour in the previously prepared mixture.
- Set aside.
- Plug in your instant pot and pour 1 cup of water in the stainless steel insert. Position a trivet on the bottom and place molds on top.
- Securely lock the lid and adjust the steam release handle. Press the "MANUAL" button and set the timer for 3 minutes.
- Cook on "High" pressure.
- When you hear the cooker's end signal, perform a quick release of the pressure. Open the pot and Let it cool completely before serving.

Nutrition:

- Calories - 427
- Fat - 32.1g
- Carbs - 0.9g
- Protein - 31.5g

GRANOLA CRUMBLE

Serving: 4

Ingredients:

- 3 tablespoon maple syrup
- 2 tablespoon apple juice
- ¼ teaspoon salt
- 4 green apples
- 7 oz. granola
- ¼ teaspoon ground cardamom
- 1 tablespoon butter

Directions:

- Peel the green apples and cut them into halves.
- Remove the seeds from the apples and chop into the small pieces.
- Place the chopped green apples in the slow cooker and add salt, apple juice, maple syrup, ground cardamom, and butter. Add the granola and stir everything together well.
- Close the slow cooker lid and cook the Granola Crumble for 4.5 hours on LOW.
- When the crumble is done,

Nutrition:

- Calories - 427
- Fat - 18.7
- Carbs - 62.48
- Protein - 5

CASSEROLE BREAKFAST

Serving: 2

Ingredients:

- 2 large eggs
- Pinch of salt
- Pinch of black pepper
- ¼ teaspoon thyme
- ¼ teaspoon garlic powder
- ¼ teaspoon onion powder
- 2 tablespoons milk
- ¼ cup Greek yogurt
- ¼ cup mushrooms, diced
- ½ cup ham, diced
- ½ cup baby spinach
- ½ cup Monterey Jack cheese, shredded
- Non-stick cooking spray

Directions:

- In a medium mixing bowl, crack the eggs and add the salt, pepper, thyme, garlic powder, onion powder, milk, and yogurt.
- Whisk all the ingredients together.

- Stir the mushrooms, ham, cheese, and spinach into the bowl.
- Spray the slow cooker with non-stick spray and pour the egg mixture into it.
- Cover, and set the temperature to HIGH. Cook for 1 ½ to 2 hours.
- Remove the casserole carefully from the cooker and slice it before serving.

Nutrition:

- Calories - 243
- Fat - 13 g
- Carbs - 10 g
- Protein - 52 g

BREAKFAST BREAD

Serving: 8

Ingredients:

- 1 tablespoon hazelnuts, chopped
- 2 pecans, chopped
- 1 egg, beaten
- 1 teaspoon ground cinnamon
- 3 tablespoons butter, softened
- 1 teaspoon baking powder
- 1 teaspoon lemon juice
- 1 ½ cup almond flour
- ½ cup coconut flour
- 2 tablespoons cream cheese
- ½ teaspoon salt

Directions:

- Place all the ingredients from the list above in the mixing bowl.
- Knead the soft but non-sticky dough.
- Let the dough rest for 10 minutes in a warm place.
- Meanwhile, line the crockpot with the baking paper.
- Place the dough in the crockpot and flatten it gently with the help of the fingertips.
- Close the crockpot lid and cook bread on High for 4 hours.
- When the time is over, open the lid and chill the bread for 15 minutes.
- Slice it into the serving.

Nutrition:

- Calories - 149
- Fat - 12.5
- Carbs - 6.9
- Protein - 4

FRUITY QUINOA MORNING

Serving: 2

Ingredients:

- 2 cups fresh fruit of your choice (berries, peaches, apples, etc.
- ¾ cup quinoa
- ⅛ teaspoon sea salt

- 1 teaspoon vanilla extract
- 3 cups water
- 2 tablespoons toasted pecans

Directions:

- In your slow cooker, combine the fruit, quinoa and salt.
- Add the vanilla extract and water.
- Stir the ingredients gently to combine well using a wooden spatula.
- Close the lid, and set the time to 8 hours on LOW.
- Divide among serving bowls and top with the toasted pecans.
- Serve warm!

Nutrition:

- Calories - 321
- Fat - 1.3 g
- Carbs - 52 g
- Protein - 11.2 g

LEEK STIR-FRY

Serving: 2

Ingredients:

- 1 cup leeks, chopped into bite-sized pieces
- 3 eggs
- 2 tbsp olive oil
- 1 tbsp butter

- Spices: 1 tsp mustard seeds
- 1 tbsp dried rosemary
- ¼ tsp chili flakes
- ¼ tsp salt

Directions:

- Rinse leeks under cold running water. Drain in a large colander and place on a clean work surface. Using a sharp knife, cut into one-inch long pieces.
- Set aside.
- Plug in the instant pot and grease the stainless steel insert with olive oil. Press the "Saute" button and add mustard seeds. Stir-fry for 2-3 minutes.
- Now add leeks and butter. Cook for 5 minutes, stirring constantly. Gently crack three eggs and season with dried rosemary, chili flakes, and salt.
- Cook until set, for approximately 4 minutes.
- Turn off the pot.
- Serve immediately.

Nutrition:

- Calories - 292
- Fat - 26.5g
- Carbs - 6g
- Protein - 9g

SWEET OATMEAL

Serving: 5

Ingredients:

- 3 cup oatmeal
- 1 cup water
- 2 cup milk
- 1/3 teaspoon salt
- 1 tablespoon brown sugar
- ¼ cup white sugar
- 1 teaspoon vanilla extract
- 1 tablespoon butter, chopped into pieces
- ¼ teaspoon ground ginger

Directions:

- Combine the water with the milk and salt.
- Add the brown sugar and white sugar.
- Stir the mixture carefully until the sugar is dissolved. After this, add vanilla extract and ground ginger.
- Stir gently. Add the oatmeal and mix everything together.
- Add butter and pour the mixture into the slow cooker.
- Close the lid and cook on HIGH for 2 hours.
- When the time is done, remove the cooked sweet oatmeal from the slow cooker and stir it carefully.
- Serve the dish immediately. Enjoy!

Nutrition:

- Calories - 217
- Fat - 8.9
- Carbs - 28.94
- Protein - 7

TOMATO COUSCOUS

Serving: 4

Ingredients:

- 1 tomato, chopped
- 1 cucumber, make slices
- 1 tablespoon olive oil
- 2 cups water
- 1 cup couscous
- 1 tablespoon lemon juice
- Salt as needed

Directions:

- Take your Instant Pot and place over dry kitchen surface; open its top lid and switch it on.
- Add the couscous and 2 cups water in the cooking pot. Add the salt and oil; stir the ingredients to combine well.
- Close its top lid and make sure that its valve it closed to avoid spillage.
- Press "MANUAL" . Adjust the timer to 15 minutes.
- Pressure will slowly build up; let the added ingredients to cook until the timer indicates zero.

- Press "CANCEL". Now press "QPR" to quickly release pressure.
- Add the vegetables. Sprinkle with some more salt; serve warm.

Nutrition:

- Calories - 76
- Fat - 3g
- Carbs - 19g
- Sodium - 18mg
- Protein - 2g

INDIAN GREENS BREAKFAST

Serving: 4

Ingredients:

- 1 pound mustard leaves
- 2 tablespoons vegetable stock
- 2 tablespoons olive oil
- 1 teaspoon ginger, grated
- 2 red onions, chopped
- 4 garlic cloves, minced
- 1 teaspoon ground cu minutes
- 1 teaspoon garam masala
- ½ teaspoon turmeric powder
- A pinch of salt and black pepper

Directions:

- In your slow cooker, combine all the ingredients, mix, cover and cook on high for 4 hours.

- Divide the mixture into bowls and serve it for breakfast.

Nutrition:

- Calories - 107
- Fat - 7,5
- Carbs - 9,2
- Protein - 3,3

BREAKFAST BREAD BOATS

Serving: 4

Ingredients:

- 6 oz. baguette
- 7 oz. breakfast sausages
- 3 tablespoons whipped cream
- 1 teaspoon minced garlic
- 1 teaspoon onion powder
- 4 oz. ham
- 6 oz. Parmesan
- 3 tablespoons ketchup
- 2 oz. green olives

Directions:

- Cut the baguette into the halves and remove the flesh from the bread.
- Chop the breakfast sausages into the tiny pieces.
- Shred Parmesan cheese and combine it with the chopped sausages.

- Add the minced garlic, onion powder, and ketchup.
- Add the whipped cream. After this, shred the ham and add it to the prepared mixture.
- Fill the baguette with the sausage mixture.
- Place the dish in the slow cooker and close the lid. Cook the dish on LOW for 5 hours.
- When the time is over, remove the dish from the slow cooker and cut every baguette half into 2 part.
- Serve the cooked dish hot!

Nutrition:

- Calories - 483
- Fat - 17.2
- Carbs - 47.06
- Protein - 35

RICOTTA AND SAUSAGE-CRUSTED PIE

Serving: 8

Ingredients:

- 1 pound Mild Sausage
- 2 cups Ricotta Cheese
- ½ cup diced Onion
- 3 tsp Olive Oil
- ¼ cup grated Parmesan Cheese
- 1 Garlic Clove, minced
- 8 cups chopped Swiss Chard
- 1 cup shredded Mozzarella Cheese

- 3 Eggs
- Salt and Pepper, to taste
- 2 cups Water

Directions:

- Heat the oil in your IP on SAUTE.
- Add onions and garlic and cook for 3 minutes.
- Add chard and cook for a couple of minutes, or until it becomes wilted.
- Season with some salt and pepper and Beat the eggs in a bowl and stir in the cheeses.
- Roll out the sausage and press it firmly into the bottom of a greased baking dish.
- Top with the chard mixture.
- Pour the cheesy egg mixture over.
- Pour the water into the IP and lower the trivet.
- Cover the pie dish with a foil and place it inside the IP.
- Close the lid and cook for 25 minutes.
- Release the pressure naturally and uncover.
- Close the lid again and cook uncovered for another 5-10 minutes.
- Serve and enjoy!

Nutrition:

- Calories - 344
- Fat - 27g
- Carbs - 4g
- Protein - 23g

SPINACH EGGS MORNING

Serving: 2

Ingredients:

Directions:

- Take your Instant Pot and place over dry kitchen surface; open its top lid and switch it on.
- Press "SAUTe".
- In its cooking pot, add and heat the oil.
- Add the beef; break into small pieces and cook for 4-5 minutes to evenly brown.
- Set the meat aside.
- In its cooking pot, add the onions; cook for 3-4 minutes until turn Add the spinach and 1 cup water.
- Close its top lid and make sure that its valve it closed to avoid spillage.
- Press "MANUAL". Adjust the timer to 3 minutes.
- Pressure will slowly build up; let the added ingredients to cook until the timer indicates zero.
- Press "CANCEL". Now press "QPR" to quickly release pressure.
- Open the top lid, mix the cooked beef.
- Press "SAUTe"; stir-fry the mix for 2 more minutes.
- Add the eggs on top and season. Cook until the eggs are cooked well.
- Serve the recipe warm.

Nutrition:

- Calories - 344
- Fat - 19g
- Carbs - 9g
- Sodium - 324mg
- Protein - 35g

VEGETABLES AND VEGAN

EGGPLANT PARMIGIANA

Serving: 8

Ingredients:

- 4
- pounds
- eggplant
- 1 tablespoon salt
- 3 large eggs
- ¼ cup milk of choice
- 1½ cup breadcrumbs
- 3 ounces Parmesan cheese
- 2 teaspoons Italian seasoning
- 4 cups marinara sauce, divided
- 1 pound
- mozzarella cheese, sliced or shredded
- Fresh basil, for topping

Directions:

- 4 medium red potatoes, cut into ½-inch cubes
- Whisk together the eggs and milk. In a separate bowl, mix the breadcrumbs and parmesan cheese.
- Peel and cut the eggplant into equal size rounds.
- Season the eggplant with salt and pepper.
- Dip the eggplant rounds into the egg-and-milk mixture, then into the breadcrumbs mixed with the parmesan cheese.
- Pour 2 cups of the marinara sauce into the slow cooker.
- Place the breaded eggplant slices in the slow cooker. Add a layer of mozzarella and another cup of the marinara sauce. Repeat the layers using the remaining eggplant rounds.
- Sprinkle the top with the remaining mozzarella and cook on low for 8 hours.
- Serve with the fresh basil.

Nutrition:

- Calories - 258
- Fat - 12 g
- Carbs - 23 g
- Protein - 16 g

EGGPLANT IN CHILI SAUCE

Serving: 3

Ingredients:

- 1 large eggplant; sliced

- 1 tablespoon lemon juice; freshly squeezed
- 1 cup sour cream
- 1-egg
- 1 tablespoon olive oil
- 3 garlic cloves; peeled
- 1 tablespoon Greek yogurt
- 1/4 teaspoon dried thyme; ground.
- 1/4 teaspoon dried oregano; ground.
- 1 teaspoon onion powder
- 1 teaspoon chili powder
- 1 teaspoon salt

Directions:

- Combine sour cream, garlic, lemon juice, Greek yogurt, egg, and all spices in a food processor. Blend until smooth and creamy, Set aside.
- Plug in the instant pot and grease the stainless steel insert with olive oil. Press the "SAUTE" button and spread the eggplant slices. Sprinkle with some salt and cook for 3-4 minutes on each side, or until lightly brown. Remove to a bowl and cover with a lid, Set aside.
- Pour in the previously prepared mixture to the instant pot. Close the lid and adjust the steam release handle. Press the "MANUAL" button and set the timer for 3 minutes. Cook on "HIGH" pressure.
- When done; perform a quick pressure release by moving the valve to the "VENTING" position and open the pot.
- Drizzle the eggplants with the sauce and sprinkle with some green onions before serving.

Nutrition:

- Calories - 418
- Fat - 34.1g
- Carbs - 13.5g
- Protein - 10.4g

HASH BROWN CASSEROLE

Serving: 6-8

Ingredients:

- Cooking spray
- 2 cups sour cream
- 1 10.75-ounce can
- condensed
- cream of mushroom soup, undiluted
- 2 cups Colby cheese, shredded
- ½ cup diced onion
- 1 32-ounce package frozen hash brown potatoes, thawed
- Salt and pepper

Directions:

- Coat the inside of a slow cooker with cooking spray.
- Mix together the sour cream, cream of mushroom soup, cheese, and onions in a large bowl.
- Add the hash browns and mix until evenly coated.
- Cook for an additional 2 1/2 hours on LOW.
- Add salt and pepper to taste then serve.

Nutrition:

- Calories - 198
- Fat - 16.2 g
- Carbs - 14.8 g
- Protein - 6.5 g

GARLIC AND PARMESAN ASPARAGUS

Serving: 2-4

Ingredients:

- 1 cup water
- 1 lb asparagus, trimmed (1 inch of the bottom
- 3 tbsp butter
- 2 cloves garlic, chopped
- Salt and ground black pepper to taste
- 3 tbsp parmesan cheese, grated

Directions:

- Pour the water into the Instant Pot and set a steam rack in the pot.
- Place the asparagus on a tin foil, add butter and garlic. Sprinkle with salt and pepper.
- Fold over the foil and seal the asparagus inside so the foil doesn't come open.
- Put the asparagus on the rack. Close and lock the lid.
- Select MANUAL and cook at HIGH pressure for 8 minutes.
- When the timer beeps, use aQuick Release.

- Carefully unlock the lid.
- Unwrap the foil packet and Sprinkle with cheese and serve.

ORIENTAL BROCCOLI

Serving: 4

Ingredients:

- 2 lb broccoli, trimmed and chopped
- 3/4 cup onion
- 1/2 tsp minced garlic
- 1/4 cup low sodium soy sauce
- 1/2 cup sliced bell pepper
- 1 Tbsp sesame seeds
- Freshly ground black pepper

Directions:

- Place the broccoli inside the slow cooker, then pour in the soy sauce.
- Add the onion, garlic, and bell pepper. Add a dash of black pepper, then toss everything to combine.
- Cover and cook for 6 hours on low.

Nutrition:

- Calories - 116

VEGGIE-NOODLE SOUP

Serving: 2

Ingredients:

- 1/2 cup chopped carrots, chopped
- 1/2 cup chopped celery, chopped
- 1 tsp Italian seasoning
- 7 oz zucchini, cut spiral
- 2 cups spinach leaves, chopped

Directions:

- Except for the zucchini and spinach, add all the ingredients to the crockpot.
- Add 3 cups of water.
- Add 1/2 cup of chopped onion
- an
- garlic, 1/8 tsp of salt and pepper and desired spices such as thyme and bay leaves if desired.
- Cover and cook for 8 hours on low.
- Add the zucchini and spinach at the last 10 minutes of cooking.

Nutrition:

- Calories - 56
- Fat - 0.5 g
- Carbs - 0.5 g
- Protein - 3 g
- Tip: Use vegetable broth instead of water for extra flavor.

KETO SOUFFLE

Serving: 6

Ingredients:

- 2 eggs
- 2-ounce softened cream cheese
- 1 cup sharp cheddar cheese
- ½ cup Asiago cheese
- ½ cup plain yogurt
- 2 tbsp. heavy cream
- 1 chopped head cauliflower
- ¼ cup minced fresh chives
- 2 tbsp. softened butter

Directions:

- Grease 1¼ quart casserole dish that will fit in an Instant Pot.
- Keep aside.
- In a food processor, add eggs, cream cheese, cheddar cheese, Asiago cheese, yogurt and heavy cream and pulse until smooth and frothy.
- Add cauliflower and pulse until chunky.
- Gently, fold in chives and butter.
- In the bottom of Instant Pot, arrange a steamer trivet and pour 1 cup of water.
- Place the casserole dish on top of the trivet.
- Secure the lid and place the pressure valve to "Seal" position.
- Select "MANUAL" and cook under "High Pressure" for about 12 minutes.

- Select the "Cancel" and carefully do a "Natural" release for about 10 minutes and then do a "Quick" release.
- Remove the lid and serve.

Nutrition:

- Calories - 234
- Fat - 17.5g
- Carbs - 1.48g
- Protein - 11.7g

ENCHILADA AMARANTH

Serving: 4

Ingredients:

- 1 cup uncooked amaranth, rinsed
- ½ cup water
- 1 small onion, diced
- 2 cloves garlic, minced
- 1 red pepper, seeds removed, diced
- 2 (15-ounce cans black beans, rinsed and drained
- 2 (10-ounce) cans red enchilada sauce
- 1 (15-ounce) can diced tomatoes
- 1 (4.5-ounce) can chopped green chilies
- 1 cup corn frozen kernels
- Juice of 1 small lime
- 1 teaspoon ground cu minutes
- 1 tablespoon chili powder
- ⅓ cup chopped cilantro
- Salt and black pepper, to taste
- 1 ½ cups shredded vegan cheese

- Optional toppings: Sliced green onions, avocado, diced tomatoes, cashew cream, cilantro, and lime wedges

Directions:

- Mix the all the ingredients EXCEPT the cheese in a 6-quart slow cooker. Mix to combine. Season with salt and pepper. Cover, and cook on HIGH for 3 hours, or on LOW 6 hours, until the amaranth is cooked.
- Remove the lid and mix the casserole. Test and adjust the spice if necessary. Stir in half the cheese, and sprinkle the other half on top. Replace the lid, and cook until the cheese has melted, about 15 minutes.
- Serve hot with the desired toppings.

Nutrition:

- Calories - 270
- Fat - 9.7 g
- Carbs - 38.1 g
- Protein - 11.6 g

VEGGIE FAJITAS

Serving: 4

Ingredients:

- 4 flour tortillas
- 4 bell peppers, any color, sliced
- 2 onions, sliced

- ½ lime, juiced
- 2 teaspoons fajita seasoning
- 2 cloves garlic, minced
- 1 tablespoon vegetable oil
- Optional toppings: Guacamole
- Salsa
- Corn, fresh
- Vegan cheddar

Directions:

- Add veggies to the slow cooker, toss in oil and seasoning. Cook on low for up to 4 hours.
- Serve on flour tortillas with chosen toppings.

Nutrition:

- Calories - 201
- Fat - 4 g
- Carbs - 36 g
- Protein - 6 g

VERITABLE FEAST CURRY

Serving: 8

Ingredients:

- 1 tbsp. coconut oil
- 1 finely chopped medium yellow onion
- 4 finely chopped garlic cloves
- 2 tbsp. curry powder
- 2½ cups cauliflower florets
- 2½ cups broccoli florets

- 3 tbsp. arrowroot starch
- Salt and freshly ground black pepper, to taste
- 2 cups water
- 1 (14-ounce) can unsweetened coconut milk
- 2 cups chopped fresh green beans

Directions:

- Place the coconut oil in the Instant Pot and select "Saute". Then add the onions for about 4-5 minutes.
- Add the garlic and curry powder and cook for about 1 minute.
- Select the "Cancel" and stir in remaining ingredients except for green beans.
- Secure the lid and place the pressure valve to "Seal" position.
- Select "MANUAL" and cook under "High Pressure" for about 20 minutes.
- Select the "Cancel" and carefully do a "Natural" release.
- Remove the lid and select "Saute".
- Stir in green beans and cook for about 5 minutes.
- Select the "Cancel" and serve immediately.

Nutrition:

- Calories - 178
- Fat - 13.9g
- Carbs - 1.7g
- Protein - 3.5g

CREAMY SCALLOPED POTATOES

Serving: 8-10

Ingredients:

- Non-stick cooking spray
- 2 tablespoons minced dried onions
- 1 medium minced garlic clove
- 8-10 medium white or red potatoes, sliced
- Salt and pepper
- 1 8-ounce package low-fat cream cheese, cubed, divided
- 1 cup shredded cheddar cheese

Directions:

- Grease the slow cooker with non-stick cooking spray.
- Mix together onions and garlic in a bowl.
- Layer ¼ of the potatoes on the bottom of the slow cooker. Sprinkle with salt and pepper, then sprinkle a bit of the onion-garlic mixture. Layer about ⅓ of the cream cheese cubes on top.
- Repeat layering of potato, salt and pepper, onion-garlic, and cream cheese.
- Cover and cook 3-4 hours on HIGH
- Stir to spread out cream cheese.
- Sprinkle top with shredded cheese.
- Cook 10 more minutes to melt cheese.

Nutrition:

- Calories - 180

- Fat - 5 g
- Carbs - 28 g
- Protein - 6 g

SOUR CREAM MUNG BEANS

Serving: 2

Ingredients:

- 1 cup mung beans sprouts
- 1 garlic clove, peeled, crushed
- ¼ teaspoon ground nutmeg
- ½ teaspoon salt
- ¾ teaspoon ground coriander
- ¼ teaspoon cumin powder
- 1 cup chicken stock
- 1 cup of water
- 1 teaspoon almond butter
- 1 tablespoon sour cream

Directions:

- Put mung beans sprouts, garlic clove, ground nutmeg, salt, ground coriander, cumin powder, chicken stock, water, almond butter and sour cream in the crockpot.
- Close the lid and cook the meal for 30 minutes on High.
- Then stir the meal very well and

Nutrition:

- Calories - 91

- Fat - 6.3
- Carbs - 6
- Protein - 4

COTTAGE PIE

Serving: 4

Ingredients:

- 3 cups mashed potatoes
- 1 cup lentils, dry
- 3 cups vegetable broth
- ½ cup red wine, dry
- 2 carrots, peeled and chopped
- 1 onion, diced
- 2 cloves garlic, minced
- ½ cup cauliflower
- 1 tablespoon tomato paste
- 1 teaspoon thyme

Directions:

- Add lentils, veggies, broth, wine, and seasoning to the slow cooker and cook covered on high for 1 hour.
- Spoon mashed potatoes over the lentils and cook on low for up to 3 hours.
- Serve warm. Finish with vegan cheddar if desired.

Nutrition:

- Calories - 374

- Fat - 3 g
- Carbs - 82 g
- Protein - 32 g

RED CABBAGE WITH GARLIC

Serving: 2-4

Ingredients:

- 1 tbsp olive oil
- ½ cup yellow onion, chopped
- 3 cloves garlic, chopped
- 6 cups red cabbage, chopped
- 1 tbsp apple cider vinegar
- 1 cup applesauce
- Salt and ground black pepper to taste
- 1 cup water

Directions:

- Preheat the Instant Pot by selecting SAUTe. Add and heat the oil.
- Add the onion and saute for about 4 minutes, until softened.
- Add the garlic and saute for 1 minute more.
- Add the cabbage, apple cider vinegar, applesauce, salt, pepper, and water.
- Press the CANCEL key to stop the SAUTe function.
- Close and lock the lid. Select MANUAL and cook at HIGH pressure for 10 minutes.
- Once timer goes off, use aQuick Release.
- Carefully unlock the lid.

- Stir the dish. Taste for seasoning and add more salt, pepper or vinegar, if needed.
- Serve.

SIMPLE PRESSURE COOKER CHICKPEA HUMMUS

Serving: 8

Ingredients:

- 1 cup dried chickpeas, soaked overnight
- 4 cloves of garlic
- 1 bay leaf
- 2 tablespoon tahini
- 1juice of lemon
- ¼ teaspoon cu minutes
- ½ teaspoon salt
- A dash of paprika
- A dash of extra virgin olive oil

Directions:

- Place the chickpeas in the Instant Pot and add 6 cups of water.
- Close the lid of the pressure cooker and press the Beans/Chili button and adjust the
- cooking time for 40 minutes.
- Do natural pressure release.
- 5. Pulse until smooth.
- 6.

Nutrition:

- Calories - 109.1
- Carbs - 0.2g
- Protein - 4.1g
- Fat - 3.8g

SIMPLE HEALTHY BEANS RECIPE

Serving: 6

Ingredients:

- 1 pound dried pinto beans, sorted, rinsed, drained
- 3 cups water
- 1 onion, chopped
- 1 bottle (18 ounces barbecue sauce
- ¼ cup molasses or honey
- ¼ teaspoon pepper

Directions:

- Soak the beans in water in a covered container overnight.
- Rinse and strain the beans.
- Combine all the ingredients in your crockpot and cook on LOW for 8 to 9 hours.

Nutrition:

- Calories - 397
- Fat - 2 g
- Carbs - 13 g
- Protein - 3 g

POTATOES AU GRATIN

Serving: 4-6

Ingredients:

- 2 tbsp butter
- ½ cup yellow onion, chopped
- 1 cup chicken stock
- 6 potatoes, peeled and sliced
- ½ cup sour cream
- 1 cup Monterey jack cheese, shredded
- Salt and ground black pepper to taste
- For the topping: 1 cup bread crumbs
- 3 tbsp melted butter

Directions:

- To preheat the Instant Pot, select SAUTe. Once hot, add the butter and melt it.
- Add the onion and saute for about 5 minutes, until softened.
- Pour in the stock and put a steam rack in the pot.
- Place the potatoes on the rack. Close and lock the lid.
- Press the CANCEL button to stop the SAUTE function, then select the MANUAL setting and set the cooking time for 5 minutes at HIGH pressure.
- In a small bowl, combine the bread crumbs and 3 tablespoon butter.
- Mix well.
- When the timer goes off, use aQuick Release.
- Carefully open the lid.

- Remove the potatoes and steam rack from the pot.
- Add the cream and cheese to the pot and stir well. Return the potatoes, season with salt and pepper and gently stir.
- Preheat the oven to broil.
- Pour the mixture in a baking dish, top with bread crumbs mix and broil for 7 minutes.
- Serve.

LOVEABLE BRUSSELS SPROUTS

Serving: 4

Ingredients:

- 2 tbsp. coconut oil
- ½ cup chopped yellow onion
- 2 tsp minced garlic
- 1 pound outer leaves removed Brussels sprout
- ½ cup water
- Salt and freshly ground black pepper, to taste

Directions:

- Place 2 tsp of the coconut oil in the Instant Pot and select "Saute". Then add the onion and garlic and cook for about 2-3 minutes.
- Select the "Cancel" and stir in the broth.
- Secure the lid and place the pressure valve to "Seal" position.
- Select "MANUAL" and cook under "Low Pressure" for about 3 minutes.

- Select the "Cancel" and carefully do a "Quick" release.
- Remove the lid and drain excess liquid.
- Serve immediately.

Nutrition:

- Calories - 115
- Fat - 7.2g
- Carbs - 3.02g
- Protein - 4.1g

CLASSIC CAULIFLOWER SPREAD WITH THYME

Serving: 6

Ingredients:

- 1-pound cauliflower; chopped into florets
- 1/2 cup canned tomatoes; sugar-free
- 1/4 cup cream cheese
- 3 tablespoon butter
- 2 tablespoon Parmesan cheese
- 2 chili peppers; diced
- 2 tablespoon apple cider vinegar
- 1/4 cup heavy cream
- 1/2 teaspoon white pepper
- 2 teaspoon dried thyme
- 1/2 red pepper flakes
- 1 teaspoon salt

Directions:

- Plug in the instant pot and grease the inner pot with butter. Press the "SAUTE" button and add peppers. Briefly cook, for 2 mintues and then add canned tomatoes. Season with salt and one teaspoon of thyme. Continue to cook for 4-5 minuts, stirring occasionally.
- Now add cauliflower and season with the remaining thyme, pepper flakes, and white pepper. Pour in one cup of water and seal the lid.
- Set the steam release handle to the "SEALING" position and press the "MANUAL" button. Cook for 12 minutes on high pressure.
- When done, perform a quick pressure release and open the lid. Chill for a while and and cider. Process until smooth a week.

Nutrition:

- Calories - 140
- Fat - 12.1g
- Carbs - 3.1g
- Protein - 4g

SOUPS AND STEWS

PIZZA SOUP

Serving: 4

Ingredients:

- 1/2 lb lean ground beef

- 7 oz unsalted diced tomatoes
- 1/2 cup chopped onion
- 1/3 cup diced green bell pepper
- 1/2 cup water
- 3/4 cup sliced mushrooms
- 13 oz low sodium spaghetti sauce
- 1/2 Tbsp Italian seasoning
- 2 oz skimmed mozzarella, shredded

Directions:

- Cook the ground beef over medium high flame in a skillet until browned. Drain the excess fat, then Stir the water, spaghetti sauce, tomatoes, onion, bell pepper, mushrooms, and Italian seasoning into the slow cooker.
- Cover and cook for 8 hours on low.
- Ladle the soup into bowls, then top with cheese and serve at once.

Nutrition:

- Calories - 293

BEEFY ONION AND BLUE CHEESE SOUP

Serving: 8

Ingredients:

- 1 ½ pounds beef steak, sliced
- 1 teaspoon salt
- 1 teaspoon black pepper

- 1 teaspoon thyme
- ¼ cup butter
- 2 cups onion, sliced
- 1 tablespoon fresh thyme
- 4 cups beef stock
- ¼ cup Worcestershire sauce
- 1 cup heavy cream
- 1 cup blue cheese, crumbled

Directions:

- Season the sliced steak with salt, black pepper, and thyme. Place the steak in a slow cooker.
- Melt the butter in a large skillet over medium-high heat.
- Once the butter has melted, add the onions and season with thyme and additional salt and pepper, if desired.
- Cook the onions, stirring frequently, for 5-7 minutes, or until they begin to caramelize.
- Add the beef stock and Worcestershire sauce to the slow cooker. Cover and cook on low for 6 hours.
- Remove the lid and stir in the heavy cream and blue cheese.
- Replace the lid and cook for an additional 30 minutes before serving.

Nutrition:

- Calories - 353.1
- Fat - 25.5 g
- Carbs - 5.2 g
- Protein - 25.6 g

VELVETY MUSHROOMS AND BROCCOLI SOUP

Serving: 8

Ingredients:

- 7 oz sliced mushrooms
- 1 2/3 lb broccoli, sliced
- 18 oz low sodium cream of mushroom soup
- 1/3 tsp thyme
- 1 3/4 cups non-fat evaporated milk
- 1/4 tsp freshly ground black pepper

Directions:

- Place the broccoli and mushrooms into the slow cooker. Add the cream of mushroom soup and evaporated milk.
- Stir in the thyme and black pepper, then cover and cook for 8 hours on low or for 4 hours on high.

Nutrition:

- Calories - 106

CLAM CHOWDER

Serving: 4

Ingredients:

- 11oz clams in juice

- 1 cup cubed bacon
- 2 cups cream
- ½ cup white wine
- 1 chopped onion
- Provence herbs
- salt and pepper

Directions:

- Cook the bacon down in your Instant Pot.
- Soften the onion in the bacon lard 5 minutes.
- Add the remaining ingredients.
- Seal and cook on Stew 15 minutes.

Nutrition:

- Calories - 400
- Fat - 35g
- Carbs - 3g
- Protein - 28g

BEEF BARLEY SOUP

Serving: 6-8

Ingredients:

- 2 tbsp olive oil
- 2 lbs beef chuck roast, cut into 1½ inch steaks
- Salt and ground black pepper to taste
- 2 onions, chopped
- 4 cloves of garlic, sliced
- 4 large carrots, chopped
- 1 stalk of celery, chopped

- 1 cup pearl barley, rinsed
- 1 bay leaf
- 8 cups chicken stock
- 1 tbsp fish sauce

Directions:

- Select the SAUTe setting on the Instant Pot and heat the oil.
- Sprinkle the beef with salt and pepper. Put in the pot and brown for about 5 minutes.
- Turn and brown the other side.
- Remove the meat from the pot.
- Add the onion, garlic, carrots, and celery. Stir and saute for 6 minutes.
- Return the beef to the pot. Add the pearl barley, bay leaf, chicken stock and fish sauce.
- Stir well.
- Close and lock the lid. Press the CANCEL button to reset the cooking program, then press the MANUAL button and set the cooking time for 30 minutes at HIGH pressure.
- Once cooking is complete, let the pressure
- Release Naturally
- for 15 minutes.
- Release any remaining steam manually. Uncover the pot.
- Remove cloves garlic, large vegetable chunks and bay leaf.
- Taste for seasoning and add more salt if needed.

ASPARAGUS AND SORREL BISQUE

Serving: 4

Ingredients:

- 1 Tbsp unsalted butter
- 1 large leek, thinly sliced, white and pale green only
- ½ tsp kosher salt or to taste
- Pepper to taste
- 1 lb asparagus, trimmed, cut into ½ inch pieces
- ¼ cup crème fraiche
- 1 Tbsp extra-virgin olive oil
- 1 stalk green garlic, sliced
- 2 cups low sodium vegetable or no chicken broth
- 2 cups sorrel or baby arugula + extra to garnish
- 1 radish, sliced, to garnish

Directions:

- Add oil and butter into a small pan and place over medium heat. Turn off the heat when the butter melts.
- Add leeks, green garlic, asparagus, salt, pepper and broth.
- Cover and cook for 2-3 hours on low or for 1 to 1 ½ hours on high or until asparagus is tender.
- Cool completely.
- Pour soup into a bowl and place in the refrigerator for 2 hours.
- Do not cover the bowl.

- Remove the chilled soup from the refrigerator and Add sorrel and blend for 40 to 50 seconds or until smooth.
- Taste and adjust the seasoning if required.
- Ladle into soup bowls. Sprinkle some pepper on top.
- Garnish with crème fraiche.
- Place radish slices on top and serve.

Nutrition:

- Calories - 153

BACON AND POTATO SOUP

Serving: 8

Ingredients:

- ½ cup bacon, pre-cooked crisp, crumbled (about 8 strips
- 2 teaspoons bacon drippings
- 1 large onion, chopped
- 3 pounds potatoes, peeled, cut into ¼-inch slices
- Non-stick cooking spray
- ½ cup water
- 2 4 ½-ounce cans chicken broth, fat-free, lower-sodium
- ½ teaspoon salt
- ½ teaspoon freshly ground black pepper
- 2 cups low-fat milk
- ¾ cup cheddar cheese, shredded
- ½ cup light sour cream
- 4 teaspoons fresh chives, chopped

Directions:

- Heat the bacon drippings in a skillet over medium heat, and stir-fry the onions until tender.
- Coat a slow cooker with non-stick spray.
- Place the potato slices in slow cooker. Scrape in the sauteed onion and drippings as well.
- Stir in the water, broth, salt, and pepper.
- Cover and cook for 8 hours on LOW or until the potatoes are tender.
- Mash potatoes. Stir in milk and cheese.
- Set slow cooker to HIGH and cook about 20 minutes longer or until heated through.
- Serve with sour cream, sprinkled with bacon and chives. Sprinkle more cheese, if desired.

Nutrition:

- Calories - 259
- Fat - 6 g
- Carbs - 38 g
- Protein - 13 g

TUSCAN CANNELLINI BEAN SOUP

Serving: 6-8

Ingredients:

- ½ pound Italian sausage
- 2 onions, chopped
- 3 cloves garlic, minced
- 2 tablespoons tomato paste
- 3½ cups chicken broth

- ½ cup dry white wine (or more chicken broth
- 1 (14½-ounce) can diced tomatoes
- 1 (15-ounce) can tomato sauce
- 2 carrots, peeled and sliced
- 3 stalks celery, sliced
- 1 green pepper, diced
- 2 tablespoons dried Italian herbs
- 2 sprigs fresh rosemary (optional)
- ½ cup roasted red peppers, diced
- ½ cup orzo, uncooked
- ½ teaspoon salt
- 1 (15-ounce) can white beans, rinsed and drained
- 2 cups baby spinach or chopped kale

Directions:

- In a large skillet, brown the sausage and then mix in the onions and garlic. When brown, Put the white wine, tomato paste, and 1 cup of chicken broth into the skillet and
- deglaze. Make sure to get the brown bits off.
- Add the liquid from the skillet and all the remaining ingredients except for the spinach to the slow cooker and cook on low for 6-8 hours.
- 20 minutes before serving, add the spinach to the slow cooker and stir well to combine.

Nutrition:

- Calories - 236
- Fat - 6.1 g
- Carbs - 25.7 g
- Protein - 16.9 g

EASY BEEF AND CABBAGE SOUP

Serving: 8

Ingredients:

- 1 cup pancetta, diced
- 2 tablespoons butter
- 2 pounds beef roast
- 1 teaspoon salt
- 1 teaspoon coarsely ground black pepper
- 6 cloves garlic, sliced
- 4 cups cabbage, sliced
- 4 cups beef stock
- 1 sprig fresh rosemary

Directions:

- Place the pancetta in a slow cooker and dot it with the butter.
- Season the beef roast with salt and coarsely ground black pepper.
- Place the roast in the slow cooker on top of the pancetta.
- Add the garlic, cabbage, beef stock, and rosemary.
- Cover, and cook on low for 10 hours.
- Remove the lid, and shred the beef roast into the soup before serving.

Nutrition:

- Calories - 325.6
- Fat - 16.1 g

- Carbs - 2.9 g
- Protein - 40.1 g

CHICKEN AND ZUCCHINI NOODLE SOUP

Serving: 8

Ingredients:

- 3 1/2 cups thinly sliced zucchini
- 3 cups chopped cooked boneless, skinless chicken
- 3/4 cup chopped celery
- 1/6 cup chopped onion
- 1/6 cup chopped carrot
- 1/6 cup coconut oil
- 10 cups low sodium chicken broth
- 1/3 tsp dried marjoram
- 2 thin slivers fresh ginger
- 1/3 tsp black pepper
- 3/4 Tbsp dried parsley
- 1 bay leaf

Directions:

- Combine the chicken, celery, onion, carrot, coconut oil, broth, marjoram, ginger, pepper, parsley, and bay leaf in the slow cooker.
- Cover and cook for 6 hours on low.
- Ladle into soup bowls and top with sliced zucchini.

Nutrition:

- Calories - 227

SUPER-GREEN SOUP

Serving: 6

Ingredients:

- 2 tbsp. butter
- 1 chopped yellow onion
- 5 crushed garlic cloves
- 1 cup chopped ham
- 4 cups homemade chicken broth
- 2 pounds halved asparagus
- ½ tsp dried thyme
- Salt and freshly ground black pepper, to taste

Directions:

- Place the butter in the Instant Pot and select "Saute". Then add the onion and cook for about 5 minutes.
- Add the garlic, ham bone and broth, and cook for about 2-3 minutes.
- Select the "Cancel" and stir in the remaining ingredients.
- Secure the lid and place the pressure valve to "Seal" position.
- Select the "Soup" and just use the default time of 45 minutes.
- Select the "Cancel" and carefully do a "Quick" release.

- Remove the lid and let the soup cool slightly.
- In a food processor, add soup in batches and pulse until smooth.
- Serve immediately.

Nutrition:

- Calories - 138
- Fat - 6.9g
- Carbs - 1.65g
- Protein - 10.7g

LEEK AND POTATO SOUP

Serving: 3

Ingredients:

- 1/2 lb small new or red potatoes, scrubbed and quartered
- 2 small leeks, white and tender greens, rinsed thoroughly and chopped
- 2 garlic cloves, minced
- 2 cups plain soy milk
- 1/3 tsp sea salt
- 1/4 tsp cracked black pepper
- 1 Tbsp mellow white miso
- 3/4 Tbsp olive oil
- Optional: 2 Tbsp toasted pine nuts

Directions:

- Place a skillet over medium flame and heat the olive oil. Saute the leeks until tender, then stir in the garlic and cook for 1 minute.
- Scrape everything into the slow cooker.
- Add the soymilk, potatoes, sea salt, and pepper into the slow cooker. Cover and cook for 3 hours on low, or until potatoes are fork tender.
- Puree the soup using a blender or immersion blender. Mix well, then adjust seasoning to taste.
- Sprinkle pine nuts on top, if desired, then serve.

Nutrition:

- Calories - 210

RABBIT CABBAGE STEW

Serving: 4

Ingredients:

- 1 whole rabbit, cleaned
- 1 cup cabbage, shredded
- 4 cups beef broth
- 3 tbsp. butter
- Spices: 1 tsp salt
- ½ tsp freshly ground white pepper
- 1 tsp cayenne pepper

Directions:

- Plug in your instant pot and combine all the ingredients in the stainless steel insert. Season with spices and stir until all well combined. Set the steam release handle and press "MANUAL" button.
- Set the timer for 35 minutes.
- When done, perform a quick release. Optionally, Serve warm.

Nutrition:

- Calories - 543
- Fat - 24.3g
- Carbs - 1.8g
- Protein - 74g

WHITE CHICKEN CHILI

Serving: 6

Ingredients:

- 1 pound ground chicken
- 2 tomatoes, chopped
- 1 green bell pepper, seeded, diced
- 1 medium onion, diced
- 4 cloves garlic, grated
- 2 tablespoons tomato paste
- 1 teaspoon oregano
- 1 teaspoon cu minutes
- 1 teaspoon salt
- 1 teaspoon black pepper

- Extra virgin olive oil

Directions:

- Brush slow cooker with extra virgin olive oil, and set slow cooker on high.
- Heat 4 tablespoons extra virgin olive oil in skillet, add ground chicken, and brown.
- Add onion, garlic, into chicken and saute for 30 seconds, place mixture in slow cooker.
- Add tomatoes, oregano, cumin, salt, black pepper into slow cooker.
- Cook on low for 7 hours.

Nutrition:

- Calories - 161
- Fat - 8 g
- Carbs - 5 g
- Protein - 17 g

GINGERED CHICKEN BROTH

Serving: 12

Ingredients:

- 1 cooked grass-fed chicken carcass (meat removed)
- 1 tbsp. peeled fresh ginger
- 1 small quartered skin-on yellow onion
- 1 cup chopped celery tops
- 2 peeled garlic cloves
- 2 tbsp. apple cider vinegar

- 12½ cups filtered water

Directions:

- In the pot of Instant Pot, add all ingredients.
- Secure the lid and place the pressure valve to "Seal" position.
- Select "MANUAL" and cook under "High Pressure" for about 60 minutes.
- Select the "Cancel" and carefully do a "Natural" release.
- Remove the lid and through a fine mesh strainer, strain the broth.
- Keep aside at room temperature to cool completely.
- Remove solidified fat from the top of the chilled broth.
- You can preserve this broth in the refrigerator for about 5-7 days or up to 3-4 months in the freezer.

Nutrition:

- Calories - 178
- Fat - 3.5g
- Carbs - 0.10g
- Protein - g

INDIAN CURRIED BROCCOLI SOUP

Serving: 6

Ingredients:

- 2 tbsp. coconut oil
- 1 chopped small yellow onion
- 3 chopped scallions
- 1 tbsp. Indian curry powder
- Salt, to taste
- 1¾ pounds broccoli florets
- 4 cups homemade chicken broth
- 1 cup full-fat unsweetened coconut milk
- Freshly ground black pepper, to taste

Directions:

- Place the coconut oil in the Instant Pot and select "Saute". Then add the onion, scallion, curry powder and pinch of salt and cook for about 5 minutes.
- Add broccoli and cook for about 1 minute
- Select the "Cancel" and stir in the broth.
- Secure the lid and place the pressure valve to "Seal" position.
- Select "MANUAL" and cook under "High Pressure" for about 5 minutes.
- Select the "Cancel" and carefully do a Natural release for about 10 minutes and then do a Quick release.
- Remove the lid and with an immersion blender, puree the soup.

- Select "Saute" and stir in coconut milk and black pepper.
- Cook for about 2-3 minutes.
- Select the "Cancel" and serve hot.

Nutrition:

- Calories - 212
- Fat - 15.6g
- Carbs - 2.31g
- Protein - 8.3g

BEST BEANS-FREE CHILI

Serving: 10

Ingredients:

- 1 tbsp. olive oil
- ½ chopped large yellow onion
- Salt, to taste
- 2½ pounds grass-fed ground beef
- 8 minced garlic cloves
- 2 (15-ounce) can sugar-free diced tomatoes with liquid
- 1 (6- ounce) can sugar-free tomato paste
- 1 (4-ounce) can green chiles with liquid
- 2 tbsp. Worcestershire sauce
- ¼ cup red chili powder
- 2 tbsp. ground cu minutes
- 1 tbsp. dried oregano
- 2 bay leaves
- Freshly ground black pepper, to taste

Directions:

- Place the oil in the Instant Pot and select "Saute". Then add the onion and salt and cook for about 10-15 minutes or until caramelized, stirring frequently.
- Add garlic and cook for about 1 minute.
- Add beef and cook for about 8-9 minutes.
- Select the "Cancel" and stir in the remaining ingredients.
- Secure the lid and select "Meat/Stew" and just use the default time of 35 minutes.
- Select the "Cancel" and carefully do a "Quick" release.
- Remove the lid and discard bay leaves.
- Serve hot.

Nutrition:

- Calories - 254
- Fat - 9.4g
- Carbs - 0.6g
- Protein - 35.6g

BEEF BORSCHT SOUP

Serving: 6

Ingredients:

- 2 pounds ground beef
- 3 beets, peeled and diced
- 3 stalks of celery, diced
- 2 large carrots, diced

- 2 cloves of garlic, diced
- 1 onion, diced
- 3 cups shredded cabbage
- 6 cups beef stock
- 1 bay leaf
- ½ tablespoon thyme
- Salt and pepper

Directions:

- Press the Saute button on the Instant Pot.
- Saute the beef for 5 minutes until slightly golden.
- Add all the rest of the ingredients in the Instant Pot.
- Close the lid and press the Manual button.
- Adjust the cooking time to 15 minutes.
- Do natural pressure release.

Nutrition:

- Calories - 477
- Carbs - 17.7g
- Protein - 44.5g
- Fat - 24.9g

CHICKEN AND BEANSPROUTS

Serving: 5

Ingredients:

- 2lbs chicken breast
- 20oz chicken stock
- 2 cups bean sprouts

- 1 red onion, cut into thin strips
- 4 green bell peppers, cut into thin strips
- 4 garlic cloves, minced
- 4 tbsp. low sodium, no soy oyster sauce

Directions:

- Mix all the ingredients in your Instant Pot.
- Set to Stew and cook for 25 minutes.
- Release the pressure quickly.

Nutrition:

- Calories - 135
- Fat - 7g
- Carbs - 10g
- Protein - 26g

FISH AND SEAFOOD

SQUID STEW

Serving: 4

Ingredients:

- 7-ounce squid rings; defrosted
- 2 cups cherry tomatoes; diced
- 1 medium-sized yellow bell pepper; sliced
- 1 small onion; finely chopped.
- 1/4 cup olive oil
- 3 cups fish stock
- 7-ounce shrimps; cleaned
- 1 cup cabbage; shredded

- 1/2 teaspoon dried oregano
- 1 teaspoon rosemary powder
- 1 teaspoon stevia powder
- 2 teaspoon pink Himalayan salt

Directions:

- Grease the inner pot with some olive oil and heat up on the "SAUTE" mode. Add onions and stir-fry until Stir in tomatoes and add about 1/4 cup of the stock. Simmer until the liquid evaporates and press the "CANCEL" button.
- Finally, add the remaining ingredients and season with oregano, rosemary, and stevia powder. Stir well and seal the lid
- Set the steam release handle to the "SEALING" position and press the "MANUAL" button set the timer for 20 minutes on high pressure.
- When done, perform a quick release and open the lid. Divide between serving plates
- and optionally sprinkle with some Parmesan. Serve and enjoy.

Nutrition:

- Calories - 279
- Fat - 15.8g
- Carbs - 8.4g
- Protein - 24.5g

SHRIMP SCAMPI

Serving: 2-4

Ingredients:

- 1 lb shrimp, peeled and deveined
- 2 tbsp olive oil
- 1 clove garlic, minced
- 1/3 cup tomato paste
- 10 oz canned tomatoes, chopped
- 1/3 cup water
- ¼ tsp oregano, dried
- 1 tbsp parsley, finely chopped
- ½ tsp kosher salt
- ½ tsp ground black pepper to taste
- 1 cup parmesan, grated

Directions:

- Preheat the Instant Pot by selecting SAUTe. Add and heat the oil.
- Add the garlic and saute for 1 minute.
- Add the shrimp, tomato paste, tomatoes, water, oregano, parsley, salt and pepper, stir.
- Close and lock the lid. Select MANUAL and cook at HIGH pressure for 3 minutes.
- When the timer goes off, use aQuick Release. Carefully open the lid.
- Sprinkle with parmesan and serve.

CREAMY MUSSEL SOUP

Serving: 4

Ingredients:

- 2 cups mussels; defrosted
- 2 tablespoon butter; unsalted
- 1 tablespoon soy sauce
- 1/4 cup Parmesan cheese
- 1-pound cauliflower; chopped into florets
- 1 cup broccoli; chopped.
- 2 cups fish stock
- 1 cup heavy cream
- 1/2 teaspoon fresh pepper; ground.
- 2 bay leaves

Directions:

- Place mussels in a large sieve and rinse thoroughly under cold running water. Drain and place in a deep bowl. Season with pepper and set aside
- Plug in the instant pot and press the "SAUTE" button. Add cauliflower and broccoli. Stir well and cook for 5 minutes.
- Now add mussels and pour in the fish stock. Drizzle with soy sauce and add bay leaves
- Seal the lid and set the steam release handle to the "SEALING" position. Press the "MANUAL" button and set the timer for 5 minutes on high pressure.
- When done, perform a quick release and open the lid. Remove the bay leaves and stir in the heavy

cream and Parmesan. Chill for a while before serving

Nutrition:

- Calories - 283
- Fat - 20g
- Carbs - 8g
- Protein - 15.9g

BALSAMIC CATFISH

Serving: 4

Ingredients:

- 2 tablespoons balsamic vinegar
- 1 tablespoon white sugar
- ¼ teaspoon salt
- ½ teaspoon ground cinnamon
- 1 teaspoon cilantro
- 1 teaspoon fish sauce
- 1 teaspoon olive oil
- 10 oz catfish

Directions:

- Pour olive oil in a skillet and preheat it until the oil starts to sizzle.
- Then put the catfish in the oil and fry for 1 minute on high heat on each side. Put the fried catfish in the slow cooker and sprinkle with the remaining olive oil from the skillet.

- Combine the balsamic vinegar, white sugar, salt, ground cinnamon, cilantro, and fish sauce.
- Mix the liquid well.
- Pour the balsamic vinegar mixture in the slow cooker and close the lid. Cook the catfish on HIGH for 45 minutes. Serve the catfish hot.
- Enjoy!

Nutrition:

- Calories - 87
- Fat - 3.3
- Carbs - 2
- Protein - 12

TILAPIA TOMATO STEW

Serving: 4

Ingredients:

- 1 (12 ounce can roasted red peppers, drained and chopped
- 1 onion, chopped
- 4 garlic cloves, minced
- 10 ounces tilapia fillets, cut into bite-sized pieces
- 1 (14.5 ounce) can diced tomatoes, undrained
- 2 tablespoons olive oil
- 1 tablespoon lemon juice
- 1 teaspoon red pepper flakes
- 1 teaspoon lemon zest
- 1 teaspoon salt
- 1 teaspoon black pepper (ground)

Directions:

- Take your Instant Pot and open the top lid.
- Add the oil and heat it; saute the onions, garlic until Add remaining ingredients; gently stir.
- Close the top lid and seal the pressure valve.
- Press "MANUAL" setting with 10 minutes of cooking time and "HIGH" pressure mode.
- Press "NPR" function to release the pressure slowly in a natural way.
- Open the lid, press "SAUTE."
- Stir-cook the mixture until thickens.
- Enjoy!

Nutrition:

- Calories - 197
- Fat - 8g
- Carbs - 11g
- Sodium - 356mg
- Protein - 7g

INSTANT POT MOK PA

Serving: 3

Ingredients:

- 3 tablespoon sticky rice, soaked in water
- 1 stalk lemongrass, sliced
- 1 small shallot, chopped
- 2 cloves of garlic, minced
- 5 Thai bird chilies
- 2 tablespoons water

- 12 kaffir lime leaves
- 2 tablespoons fish sauce
- 1 banana leaf, washed
- 2 pounds white fish fillet
- 1 tablespoon green onions
- 1 cup fresh dill leaves, chopped
- ½ cup cilantro leaves, chopped

Directions:

- Place in a mortar or food processor the rice, lemongrass, shallots, garlic, birth chilies, water, kaffir lime leaves, and fish sauce. Pulse until fine. Set aside.
- Lay down the banana leaves on a leveled surface and place fish in the middle. Pour the rice mixture on top and garnish with green onions, dill, and cilantro leaves.
- Fold the banana leaf and secure with a string. You can even wrap aluminum foil over.
- Place a steamer basket in the Instant Pot and pour water over.
- Place the fish wrapped in banana leaf on the steamer rack.
- Close the lid and press the Steam button.
- Adjust the cooking time to 15 minutes.
- Do quick pressure release.

Nutrition:

- Calories - 552
- Carbs - 16.9g
- Protein - 57.2g
- Fat - 28.2g

SHRIMP DIABLO

Serving: 4

Ingredients:

- 1 spaghetti squash (approximately 2 cups when cooked
- 1 cup onion, sliced
- 4 cloves garlic, crushed and minced
- 1 cup chicken or seafood stock
- 1 teaspoon salt
- 1 teaspoon black pepper
- 1 pound shrimp, cleaned and deveined
- ¼ cup butter, melted
- 1 tablespoon crushed red pepper flakes
- 1 teaspoon cayenne powder
- 1 teaspoon oregano
- 1 tablespoon lemon juice

Directions:

- Using a fork or sharp knife, poke 12-15 holes or small cuts in the surface of the spaghetti squash and place it in the center of the slow cooker.
- Add the onion, garlic, chicken stock, salt, and black pepper around the squash. Cover, and cook on low for 6 hours.
- Remove the spaghetti squash from the slow cooker and turn the heat to high.
- Allow the squash to cool just enough to handle before cutting it in half and scooping the insides back into the slow cooker. Discard the empty shell.

- Give the contents of the slow cooker a quick toss to mix the ingredients.
- Add the shrimp, melted butter, crushed red pepper flakes, cayenne powder, oregano, and lemon juice to the slow cooker.
- Cover and cook 10-15 minutes, or until the shrimp are cooked through.

Nutrition:

- Calories - 252.7
- Fat - 13.1 g
- Carbs - 8.7 g
- Protein - 25 g

LIGHT LOBSTER SOUP

Serving: 6

Ingredients:

- 5 cups fish stock
- 1 tablespoon paprika
- ½ teaspoon powdered chili
- 1 teaspoon salt
- 8 oz lobster tails
- 6 oz Cheddar cheese, shredded
- 1 teaspoon ground white pepper
- 1/3 cup fresh dill
- 1 tablespoon almond milk
- 1 garlic clove, peeled
- 3 potatoes

Directions:

- Pour the fish stock into the slow cooker bowl.
- Peel the potatoes and cut into cubes. Put the potato cubes in the slow cooker. Add the powdered chili, paprika, salt, ground white pepper, almond milk, and peeled garlic cloves. Close the lid and cook the liquid for 2 hours on HIGH.
- Meanwhile, chop the fresh dill. When the time is done, add the fresh dill and lobster tails.
- Close the lid and cook the soup on HIGH for 1.5 hours more. Ladle the prepared soup into the bowls and sprinkle with the shredded cheese. Enjoy!

Nutrition:

- Calories - 261
- Fat - 4.8
- Carbs - 37.14
- Protein - 19

SQUID RINGS WITH SPINACH AND POTATO

Serving: 3

Ingredients:

- 1-pound squid rings; frozen
- 2 cups cauliflower; roughly chopped
- 1-pound fresh spinach; torn
- 2 tablespoon lemon juice

- 4 tablespoon extra virgin olive oil
- 1 teaspoon dried rosemary; crushed
- 2 thyme sprigs; fresh
- 1 teaspoon garlic paste
- 1 teaspoon sea salt

Directions:

- Place squid rings in a deep bowl and pour in enough warm water to cover. Let it sit for a while. a
- large colander and drain, Set aside.
- Plug in the instant pot and grease the inner pot with two tablespoons of olive oil. Press the "SAUTE" button and add garlic paste and rosemary. Stir-fry for one minute and then add the spinach. Season with salt and cook for 3-4 minutes or until wilted. Remove the spinach from the pot and set aside.
- Add the remaining oil to the pot and heat up on the "SAUTE" mode. Add chopped cauliflower making an even layer. Top with squid rings and drizzle with lemon juice and optionally some more olive oil to taste Sprinkle with salt, add thyme sprigs, and pour in one cup of water (or fish stock)
- Seal the lid and set the steam release handle to the "SEALING" position. Press the ' "FISH" button and set the timer for 9 minutes
- When you hear the cooker's end signal, carefully move the pressure valve to the
- "VENTING" position to release the pressure

- Open the pot and stir in the spinach. Optionally, season with some more garlic powder or dried thyme. Serve and enjoy.

Nutrition:

- Calories - 353
- Fat - 21.5g
- Carbs - 8.9g
- Protein - 29.3g

CREOLE SHRIMP

Serving: 3

Ingredients:

- 3/4 cup sliced celery
- 1/3 cup chopped onion
- 4 oz unsalted tomato sauce
- 1/2 cup chopped green bell pepper
- 14 oz unsalted whole tomatoes
- 1/2 lb shrimp, peeled and deveined
- 1/4 tsp minced garlic
- 1/8 tsp pepper
- 3 drops hot pepper sauce

Directions:

- Place the onion, celery, tomato sauce, green bell pepper, garlic, pepper, and hot sauce into the slow cooker. Crush the whole tomatoes and mix in.

- Cover and cook for 2 hours on high or for 3 hours on low.
- Add the shrimp, cover and cook for an additional 1 hour on high. Best served over hot black or red rice.

Nutrition:

- Calories - 139

HERBED MOROCCAN TILAPIA

Serving: 4

Ingredients:

- 15 oz tilapia fillet
- 1 cup heavy cream
- 1 teaspoon coconut oil
- ¼ teaspoon ground cinnamon
- ¼ teaspoon cu minutes
- ¼ teaspoon turmeric
- ¼ teaspoon ginger
- ¼ teaspoon paprika
- ¼ teaspoon coriander
- ¼ teaspoon saffron
- ¾ teaspoon ground black pepper
- 1 teaspoon salt

Directions:

- In the shallow bowl, mix up together ground cinnamon, cumin, turmeric, ginger, paprika, coriander, saffron, ground black pepper, and salt.

- Rub the tilapia fillet with the spice mixture and Add heavy cream and coconut oil.
- Close the lid and cook fish for 2 hours on High.

Nutrition:

- Calories - 204
- Fat - 13.3
- Carbs - 1.5
- Protein - 20.5

CREAMY SHRIMP STEW

Serving: 4

Ingredients:

- 1-pound shrimps; peeled and deveined
- 3 bacon slices; chopped
- 1/4 cup bell peppers; diced
- 1 cup cherry tomatoes; sliced in half
- 1/2 cup heavy cream
- 1/4 cup scallions; chopped
- 2 cups fish stock
- 4 tablespoon olive oil
- 1 cup onion; finely chopped.
- 1/4 teaspoon white pepper; freshly ground.
- 2 teaspoon apple cider vinegar
- 1 teaspoon Old Bay seasoning
- 1/2 teaspoon garlic powder
- 1/2 teaspoon salt

Directions:

- Plug in the instant pot and press the "SAUTE" button. Grease the inner pot with olive oil and add bacon. Cook for 3-4 minutes or until lightly golden brown and crisp. Remove the bacon from the pot and set aside.
- Now add onions and bell peppers. Cook until Now add shrimps and give it a good stir. Pour in the remaining stock and season with Old Bay seasoning, garlic powder, salt, and pepper. Sprinkle with some apple cider and seal the lid.
- Set the steam release handle to the "SEALING" position and press the "MANUAL" button. Cook for 8 minutes on high pressure
- When done, release the pressure naturally and open the lid. Serve and enjoy.

Nutrition:

- Calories - 427
- Fat - 28.5g
- Carbs - 6.4g
- Protein - 35g

BROCCOLI SALMON

Serving: 2

Ingredients:

- 2 tablespoons low-sodium soy sauce
- 2 tablespoons maple syrup
- 2 tablespoons lemon juice

- 1 pound broccoli florets
- 2 medium-sized salmon fillets
- Salt and pepper to taste

Directions:

- In a mixing bowl, thoroughly combine the soy sauce, maple syrup, and lemon juice.
- Arrange the broccoli and the salmon in the slow cooker, and season with salt and pepper.
- Top with the sauce, and stir gently to combine.
- Cover, and cook on LOW for 3 hours.
- Serve hot, and enjoy!

Nutrition:

- Calories - 331
- Fat - 9.2 g
- Carbs - 11.6 g
- Protein - 23 g

SEAFOOD PAELLA

Serving: 6

Ingredients:

- 1 teaspoon extra-virgin olive oil
- 1½ pounds boneless skinless chicken breasts, cubed
- ½ pound sliced chorizo
- Kosher salt and freshly ground black pepper, to taste
- 1 cup uncooked long-grain rice

- 1 (15-ounce can diced tomatoes, undrained
- 1 large yellow onion, peeled and chopped
- 4 cloves garlic, peeled and minced
- 2 teaspoons paprika
- ¼ teaspoon cayenne pepper
- 2 cups reduced-sodium chicken broth
- ⅓ cup dry white wine
- ½ pound raw medium shrimp, peeled and deveined
- 1½ cups frozen peas, thawed and drained
- Fresh parsley, chopped, for garnish
- Lemon wedges, for serving

Directions:

- In a large skillet, heat olive oil over medium-high heat. When the skillet is hot, add the chicken and chorizo. Cook until chicken is brown and chorizo is cooked.
- Add the uncooked rice, tomatoes, onion, garlic, and all of the spices, followed by the chicken broth and wine. Stir a couple of times to mix well.
- Cook on high for an hour and a half, then add the shrimp and the peas. Stir those in,
- then cook for 30 more minutes.
- Serve when the shrimp is cooked through.

Nutrition:

- Calories - 274
- Fat - 11 g
- Carbs - 22 g
- Protein - 21.7 g

ADOBO SHRIMPS RECIPE

Serving: 4

Ingredients:

- 1-pound shrimps; peeled and deveined
- 2 tablespoon green onions; finely chopped
- 2 cups fish stock
- 1/4 cup soy sauce
- 1/4 cup olive oil
- 1/4 cup rice vinegar
- 1 small onion; finely chopped
- 1 red chili pepper; finely chopped.
- 5 garlic cloves; crushed
- 2 tablespoon fish sauce
- 1 tablespoon peppercorn
- 1 teaspoon stevia powder
- 2 teaspoon salt

Directions:

- In a large bowl, whisk together olive oil, rice vinegar, soy sauce, green onions, garlic, fish sauce, chopped onion, chili pepper, salt, peppercorn, and stevia
- Add shrimps and give it a good stir making sure to coat shrimps well in the marinade. a
- large Ziploc bag and refrigerate for at least 30 minutes (up to 2 hours)
- Plug in the instant pot and pour in the stock. Remove the shrimps from the Ziploc and place in the pot along with 1/4 cup of the marinade

- Stir well and seal the lid. Set the steam release handle to the "SEALING" position and press the "MANUAL" button
- Set the timer for 10 minutes. When done, perform a quick release and serve immediately.

Nutrition:

- Calories - 298
- Fat - 15.5g
- Carbs - 5.7g
- Protein - 30.4g

TUNA SALPICAO

- 1 chili pepper
- 2 oz olive oil
- 1-pound tuna fillet
- 1 teaspoon salt
- 2 oz garlic cloves
- ½ teaspoon sage

Directions:

- Pour the olive oil and black peas in the slow cooker bowl and add salt.
- Chop the chili pepper and peel the garlic cloves. Slice the garlic. Add the chopped
- chili pepper and sliced garlic cloves.
- Add sage and stir the oil mixture.
- Close the slow cooker lid and cook it on LOW for 40 minutes.
- Chop the tuna into cubes and add into the slow cooker. Cook the meat for 20 minutes on HIGH.

Then remove the tuna from the slow cooker and Sprinkle it with the oil fragrant mixture. Serve it!

Nutrition:

- Calories - 249
- Fat - 15.4
- Carbs - 5.88
- Protein - 23

KETO SEAFOOD STEW

Serving: 5

Ingredients:

- 2 -pounds sea bass fillets; cut into chunks
- 7-ounce shrimps; peeled and deveined
- 2 small tomatoes; roughly chopped.
- 3 tablespoon soy sauce
- 1 large onion; finely chopped
- 5 cups fish stock
- 4 tablespoon olive oil; extra-virgin
- 3 celery stalks; finely chopped
- 2 bay leaves
- 1 teaspoon black pepper; freshly ground.
- 1 tablespoon Creole seasoning
- 2 teaspoon sea salt

Directions:

- Clean and rinse fish fillets. Pat dry with some kitchen paper and set aside.

- In a small bowl, combine Creole seasoning with salt and pepper. Rub the fish with this mixture making sure to coat on all sides.
- Plug in the instant pot and press the "SAUTE" button. Grease the inner pot with olive oil and heat up. Add the prepared fish and cook for 4-5 minutes, stirring occasionally.
- When the fish has nicely browned, gently remove from the pot and set aside
- Grease the inner pot with some more oil and add onions and celery stalk. Season with some salt and stir well. Continue to cook for 2-3 minutes
- Now press the "CANCEL" button and add the fish, shrimps, and tomatoes. Drizzle with soy sauce and pour in the stock.
- Seal the lid and set the steam release handle to the "SEALING" position. Press the "MANUAL" button and set the timer for 5 minutes on high pressure
- When done; release the pressure naturally and open the lid. Optionally, stir in some fresh parsley and serve.

Nutrition:

- Calories - 433
- Fat - 18.5g
- Carbs - 4.6g
- Protein - 58.5g

SEAFOOD JAMBALAYA

Serving: 4

Ingredients:

- 14 oz diced tomatoes, not drained
- 1 small yellow onion, chopped
- 2 celery ribs, sliced thinly
- 7 oz crushed tomatoes
- 1 bell pepper, seeded and chopped
- 3 garlic cloves, minced
- 1/2 tsp dried oregano
- 1/2 tsp sweet paprika
- 1/4 tsp hot pepper sauce
- 1/4 tsp cayenne pepper
- 1/4 tsp cracked black pepper
- 1/3 tsp sea salt
- 1/3 tsp dried thyme
- 1/3 tsp dried oregano
- 1/2 bay leaf
- 1/4 cup chopped fresh parsley
- 1/2 lb fresh shrimp, shelled and deveined
- 1/2 lb fresh bay scallops
- 1 1/2 cups cooked long grain brown rice
- Juice and zest of 1/2 lemon
- A dash of xylitol

Directions:

- Mix together the onion, tomatoes, celery, peppers, bay leaf, garlic, lemon zest, thyme, paprika, oregano, hot sauce, peppers, sea salt, and xylitol.

- Cover and cook for 3 hours on high or for 6 hours on low.
- Set heat to high, then stir in the scallops and shrimp. Cover and cook again for 15 minutes, or until the seafood is cooked through.
- Stir in the parsley and lemon juice, then spoon on top of the cooked brown rice and serve.

Nutrition:

- Calories - 236

BUTTERY SALMON WITH ONIONS AND CARROTS

Serving: 4

Ingredients:

- 4 salmon fillets
- 4 tablespoons butter
- 4 onions, chopped
- 16 ounces baby carrots
- 3 cloves garlic, minced
- Salt and pepper

Directions:

- Melt butter in the microwave, and pour into the slow cooker.
- Add onions, garlic, and baby carrots.
- Cover and cook for 6-7 hours on LOW, stirring occasionally until vegetables begin to caramelize.

- Place fillet over vegetables in slow cooker, and season with salt and pepper.
- Cover and cook on LOW for 1-2 hours until salmon flakes.
- Serve on a serving plate, and top with onion mixture.

Nutrition:

- Calories - 367
- Fat - 22 g
- Carbs - 12.2 g
- Protein - 39 g

CHICKEN AND POULTRY

KUNG PAO CHICKEN

Serving: 2

Ingredients:

- 1 ½ pound Chicken skinless chicken breast; cut into 1-inch cubes.
- 1/2 red bell pepper diced
- 1/2 cup onion chopped red or white
- 2 tablespoon vegetable oil
- 1 zucchini diced
- 3 garlic cloves minced.
- Green onion to garnish
- For the sauce
- 1/2 teaspoon red pepper flakes
- 1/4 teaspoon ground black pepper
- 2/3 cup garlic coconut aminos

- 1/2 teaspoon ground ginger.

Directions:

- Add oil to instant pot and sauteed chicken until lightly browned
- Add vegetables, stir. Add sauces and lid, set to seal.
- Cook on meat for 30 minutes on LOW pressure or 15 minutes on high. Release and
- serve hot

Nutrition:

- Calories - 450
- Protein - 53g
- Fat - 24g
- Fat - 6g

SLOW CHICKEN CURRY

Serving: 2

Ingredients:

- 2 chicken breasts
- 1 cup white kidney beans
- ½ cup sweet onion, thinly sliced
- ¼ cup red pepper, chopped
- ½ cup peach salsa
- 2 teaspoons curry powder
- Salt and pepper to taste
- ½ cup green beans
- 1 tablespoon cornstarch

- ½ cup water
- Hot cooked rice, for serving

Directions:

- Place the chicken, kidney beans, onion, and red pepper in the slow cooker.
- In a mixing bowl, combine the peach salsa, curry powder, salt, and pepper. Mix and pour over the chicken.
- Cover and cook for 4-5 hours until the chicken is cooked through and tender.
- Add the green beans and stir.
- Mix the cornstarch with the water, and slowly pour it into the slow cooker. Stir.
- Cover, and cook for 30 minutes on HIGH.

Nutrition:

- Calories - 486
- Fat - 6 g
- Carbs - 59 g
- Protein - 46 g

LEMON SAUCE PULLED CHICKEN

Serving: 11

Ingredients:

- 23 oz chicken breast, boneless
- 1 lemon
- 1 tablespoon cornstarch
- 1 teaspoon salt

- 1 cup heavy cream
- 1 tablespoons flour
- 1 teaspoon ground black pepper
- 1 teaspoon minced garlic
- 1 tablespoon mustard
- 3 tablespoons lemon juice
- 1 red onion

Directions:

- Grate the lemon zest from the lemon and squeeze the juice.
- Combine the prepared ingredients with the salt, minced garlic, lemon juice, and ground black pepper. Chop the chicken breast and sprinkle with the lemon mixture.
- Peel the onion and grate it. Add the grated onion to the chicken and leave it for 15 minutes to marinate.
- Meanwhile, combine the mustard, heavy cream, and flour.
- Whisk until the mixture is smooth. After this, add the cornstarch and stir it carefully again. Put the mixture on the low heat and simmer it for 10 minutes.
- Stir it constantly.
- When you get the thick sauce, it is cooked. Put the chicken in the slow cooker bowl and sprinkle it with the all remaining lemon mixture.
- Close the slow cooker and cook the dish on HIGH for 3 hours. Add the heavy cream sauce and close the lid.

- Cook the chicken on LOW for 4 hours more. Shred the prepared chicken and stir the mixture well.
- Serve the chicken hot. Enjoy!

Nutrition:

- Calories - 154
- Fat - 9.6
- Carbs - 3.59
- Protein - 13

GLAZED DUCK BREAST

Serving: 2

Ingredients:

- 1 lb. duck breast, chopped into bite-sized pieces
- 1 tbsp. olive oil
- 3 cups chicken broth
- 1 tbsp. Dijon mustard
- 1 tsp honey
- ¼ cup apple cider vinegar
- Spices: 1 tsp salt
- ½ tsp pepper
- 1 tsp garlic powder

Directions:

- Remove the meat from the refrigerator about one hour before cooking.
- Rub the meat with onion powder and place in your instant pot along with the chicken broth.

Seal the lid and press the "MEAT" button. When you hear the cooker's end signal, perform a quick release and open the lid. Remove the meat from the pot along with the broth.
- Press the "SAUTE" button and grease the stainless steel insert with oil. Add apple cider, Dijon, and honey. Sprinkle with salt and pepper and cook for 3-4 minutes.
- Add the meat and coat well.
- Serve immediately.

Nutrition:

- Calories - 398
- Fat - 15g
- Carbs - 4.7g
- Protein - 55.7g

CHICKEN SATAY

Serving: 5

Ingredients:

- 1 tablespoon peanut butter
- 1 teaspoon salt
- 15 oz chicken fillet, chopped
- 1 teaspoon chili flakes
- ½ cup of coconut milk
- ¼ cup heavy cream
- 1 onion, sliced
- 1 red bell pepper, sliced
- ½ cup of water
- ½ teaspoon minced ginger

- 1 teaspoon apple cider vinegar

Directions:

- Put all ingredients from the list above in the crockpot and gently mix with the help of the spoon.
- Close the crockpot lid and cook the satay overnight (for 9 hours.
- When chicken satay is cooked, let it chill to the room temperature and then

Nutrition:

- Calories - 274
- Fat - 15.9
- Carbs - 6.1
- Protein - 26.6

GARLIC LEMON CHICKEN

Serving: 4

Ingredients:

- 6-8 boneless chicken thighs (skinless)
- 2 tablespoons olive oil
- 3 tablespoons butter; divided
- 1 small onion; chopped.
- 4 garlic cloves; sliced or minced.
- 1/2 teaspoon garlic powder.
- 1 ½ tablespoons Italian seasoning
- Chopped fresh parsley and lemon slices for garnish; if desired.

- Juice and zest of one lemon
- 1/3 cup homemade or low sodium chicken broth
- sea salt and pepper; to taste

Directions:

- Season chicken with salt, pepper and garlic powder.
- Press the Saute function (Normal setting) on the Instant Pot and add the olive oil to the pot.
- Place chicken in the Instant Pot and allow to sear on each side for 2 minutes, or until golden brown. This helps to seal in the juices and keep it tender
- Once browned, remove from Instant Pot and set aside.
- Melt butter in Instant Pot and stir in the onions and garlic. Add lemon juice to deglaze pan
- Cook for 1 minute then add Italian seasoning, lemon zest, and chicken broth.
- Place the chicken back into the Instant Pot, lock the lid, and turn the valve to SEAL.
- Select the Manual (older models) or Pressure Cook (newer models) button and adjust the timer to 8 minutes
- It will take about 5-10 minutes to come to pressure and start counting down.
- When done, allow to naturally release for 3 minutes then using a long spoon push the valve to RELEASE, then remove your Instant Pot lid.
- Sprinkle with chopped parsley and serve hot with your favorite sides. Spoon sauce over chicken and garnish with lemon slices, if desired

Nutrition:

- Calories - 500
- Fat - 15g
- Protein - 56g
- Carbs - 6g

CREAMY MEXICAN CHICKEN

Serving: 4

Ingredients:

- 5 boneless chicken breasts
- 1 15½-ounce can corn
- 1 15-ounce jar salsa
- 1 8-ounce package cream cheese, cut into chunks
- 1 15½-ounce can black beans
- Cooking spray
- Salt and pepper

Directions:

- Spray slow cooker with cooking spray.
- Place boneless chicken breasts into slow cooker. Season with salt and pepper.
- Add salsa, black beans, and drained corn.
- Cover. Put on HIGH for 4 hours.
- Add cream cheese, and let it sit for ½ hour. Or until the cream cheese has melted.
- Serve.

Nutrition:

- Calories - 308
- Fat - 34.2 g
- Carbs - 48 g
- Protein - 68.3 g

CREAMY GARLIC TUSCAN CHICKEN THIGHS

Serving: 4

Ingredients:

- 4 chicken thighs; fat trimmed
- 4 -ounce reduced-fat cream cheese
- 2 ½ cups fresh spinach
- 1/4 cup Parmigiano Reggiano cheese; grated
- 3 garlic cloves; chopped
- 1 teaspoon olive oil
- 1/4 cup sun-dried tomatoes
- 1 tablespoon Better Than Bouillon Chicken Seasoning
- 1 cup low-sodium chicken broth
- 1 cup unsweetened almond milk
- 2 tablespoon heavy whipping cream
- 2 teaspoon Italian seasoning
- 1 teaspoon cornstarch
- 1 teaspoon water
- Salt; pepper; to taste

Directions:

- Rinse the chicken and pat dry. Season with Italian seasoning, salt, and pepper
- Turn Instant Pot on to "SAUTE" setting. Once hot, add the olive oil
- Place the chicken in the Instant Pot and brown, 2-3 minutes on each side
- Stir in the chicken broth, milk, Better Than Bouillon, and remaining Italian seasoning
- Close the lid and seal. Cook on "MANUAL" (High Pressure), adjusting cooking time to 14 minutes
- Once cooking is finished, allow quick release of steam
- Open the pot and remove the chicken.
- Add the sun-dried tomatoes, cream cheese, whipping cream, parmigiano Reggiano, garlic, and spinach to the pot. Turn the Instant Pot on to "SAUTE".
- Cook for 3-4 minutes to melt the cheese.
- Mix the cornstarch and water in a small bowl. Add it to the pot and stir
- Place chicken on a serving dish and garnish with the sauce, Serve.

Nutrition:

- Calories - 246
- Carbs - 6 g
- Carbs - 1.7 g
- Fat - 20 g
- Protein - 10 g

CHICKEN FAJITA

Serving: 5

Ingredients:

- ½ can (from a 14.5 oz can diced tomatoes with chilies
- ½ yellow bell pepper, julienned
- ½ red bell pepper, julienned
- ½ orange bell pepper, julienned
- ½ green bell pepper, julienned
- 3 cloves garlic, minced
- 1 medium onion, julienned
- 1 ¼ lb chicken breasts, skinless, boneless
- 1 tsp ground cu minutes
- ¼ tsp salt or to taste
- ½ tsp smoked paprika
- Lime wedges to serve (optional)
- ¼ tsp freshly ground black pepper
- Cooking spray

Directions:

- Spray the inside of the slow cooker pot with cooking spray.
- Add half the tomatoes into the slow cooker. Spread it evenly. Place half the peppers and half the onions over the tomatoes. Sprinkle garlic all over the peppers.
- Place chicken over the peppers.
- Mix together cumin, paprika, pepper and salt in a bowl and sprinkle over the chicken.

- Layer with remaining tomatoes over the chicken followed by remaining peppers and onion.
- Cover and cook for 6-7 hours on low or for 3-4 hours on high.
- Serve over low carb tortillas or lettuce leaves with lime wedges if using.

Nutrition:

- Calories - 251

ROSEMARY CHICKEN WITH BACON

Serving: 6

Ingredients:

- 2 lbs. chicken breast, boneless and skinless, sliced into 1-inch thick slices
- 8 garlic cloves
- 6 bacon slices
- Spices: 1 teaspoon rosemary
- ½ tsp Himalayan salt
- ¼ tsp freshly ground black pepper
- 2 tbsp. oil
- 3 cups chicken broth

Directions:

- Grease the bottom of your stainless steel insert with oil. Add bacon and season with salt.
- Press "Sautee" button. Cook for 3 minutes.

- Meanwhile, place the meat in a separate dish. Using a sharp knife, make 8 incisions into the meat and place a garlic clove in each. Rub the meat with spices and Press "Cancel" button and pour in the chicken broth. Seal the lid and set the steam release handle.
- Set the "MANUAL" mode for 25 minutes.
- When done, press "Cancel" button and perform a natural pressure release.
- Serve warm.

Nutrition:

- Calories - 441
- Fat - 23.3g
- Carbs - 2g
- Protein - 52.3g

GARAM MASALA CHICKEN

Serving: 4

Ingredients:

- 2 lbs chicken breasts, skinless and boneless
- 1 cup heavy cream
- ½ cup cherry tomatoes, diced
- 1 small onion, diced
- 3 cups chicken broth
- 2 tbsp vegetable oil
- Spices: 1 tsp garam masala powder
- 1 tsp cumin powder
- 1 tsp coriander powder
- 1 tsp cayenne pepper, ground

- ½ tsp salt
- ½ tsp black pepper, ground

Directions:

- Rinse the chicken breasts under cold running water and pat dry with a kitchen paper.
- Cut into bite-sized pieces and set aside.
- Plug in your instant pot and grease the stainless steel insert with vegetable oil. Add chicken pieces and sprinkle with salt and pepper. Cook for 5 minutes, or unil
- lightly browned.
- Remove the chicken to a plate and set aside.
- Add onions and cherry tomatoes. Add all the remaining spices and stir-fry for 5 minutes. Pour in the heavy cream and broth. Stir well and finally add the chicken.
- Securely lock the lid. Adjust the steam release handle and press the "MANUAL" button. Set the timer for 10 minutes and cook on "High" pressure.
- When you hear the cooker's end signal, perform a quick release of the pressure and open the pot.

Nutrition:

- Calories - 638
- Fat - 36g
- Carbs - 3.8g
- Protein - 70.4g

GAME DAY BUFFALO WINGS

Serving: 4

Ingredients:

- 2 pounds chicken wings
- 1 teaspoon salt
- 1 teaspoon black pepper
- 2/3 cup hot sauce (preferably Frank's Red Hot
- 1/2 cup butter
- 1 tablespoon apple cider vinegar
- 1/4 teaspoon Worcestershire sauce
- 1 garlic clove, minced
- 1/2 cup water

Directions:

- Season the chicken wings with salt and pepper.
- Combine hot sauce, butter, vinegar, Worcestershire sauce, garlic, and water in the Instant Pot. Put the steamer basket in place and arrange the wings in it.
- Close the lid and set cooking time for 5 minutes. Use quick release to remove the steam.
- Remove the steamer basket with the wings. Set the pot to Saute mode and reduce the sauce to your desired consistency.
- Toss the wings with the sauce and serve with blue cheese dressing.

Nutrition:

- Calories - 498

- Fat - 31.36 g
- Carbs - 1.14 g
- Protein - 50.69 g

SHREDDED CHICKEN WITH SHIITAKE

Serving: 5

Ingredients:

- 6 shiitake mushrooms
- 1 lb chicken breast, boneless and skinless
- 1 ½ cup chicken stock
- 1 spring onion, finely chopped
- 4 tbsp sesame oil
- 2 tbsp butter
- 2 tbsp dark soy sauce
- 1 tbsp light soy sauce
- ½ tsp stevia powder
- 2 tsp rice vinegar
- Spices: 1 tbsp fresh ginger, grated
- ½ tsp pepper, freshly ground
- ½ tsp chili flakes

Directions:

- In a small bowl, whisk together oil, dark soy sauce, light soy sauce, stevia powder, rice vinegar, ginger, chili flakes, and pepper.
- Optionally, add some salt and set aside.
- Rinse the meat and place on a cutting board. Chop into smaller pieces and place at the bottom of your instant pot.

- Add spring onions and pour in the stock.
- Seal the lid and set the steam release handle to the "Sealing" position.
- Press the "Poultry" button and cook for 10 minutes.
- When you hear the cooker's end signal, perform a quick pressure release and open the lid. Remove the chicken from the pot and place in a deep bowl. Drizzle with the prepared soy mixture and shred with two forks.
- Set aside.
- Remove the remaining stock from the pot and press the "Saute" button.
- Grease the inner pot with butter and heat up.
- Add shiitake and briefly cook - for 3-4 minutes, stirring constantly.
- Now add the meat and give it a good stir.
- Cook for another 5 minutes.
- When done, remove from the pot and serve immediately.

Nutrition:

- Calories - 299
- Fat - 18.1g
- Carbs - 11.3g
- Protein - 21.7g

CHICKEN AND PINEAPPLE

Serving: 8

Ingredients:

- 6 boneless, skinless chicken breasts
- 30 oz canned pineapple chunks, not drained
- 3 Tbsp low sodium soy sauce or coconut aminos
- 2 cloves garlic, minced
- 12 oz canned sliced water chestnuts, drained
- 1 1/2 tsp grated fresh ginger
- 2 red bell peppers, chopped
- 1/2 cup honey or liquid noncaloric sweetener
- 1 1/2 Tbsp cornstarch

Directions:

- Combine the pineapple juice, garlic, honey or sweetener, soy sauce, ginger, and cornstarch in a bowl.
- Put the pineapples, water chestnuts, and chicken breasts into the slow cooker, then pour the pineapple juice mixture all over and turn to coat.
- Cover and cook for 6 hours on low.
- Remove the lid, stir in the bell peppers, and cook for an additional half hour.
- Best served with wild or brown rice (not included in the calorie count.

Nutrition:

- Calories - 255

WHITE CHICKEN CHILI

Serving: 8

Ingredients:

- 10 medium chicken thighs; boneless, skinless, cubed
- 1 medium onion; diced.
- 2 tablespoon butter
- 1 (14)-ounce can green chiles; diced.
- 2 teaspoon salt
- 2 teaspoon cu minutes
- 2 teaspoon oregano
- 1 teaspoon black pepper
- 1-pound frozen cauliflower
- 4 cups chicken broth
- 2 cups sour cream
- 1 cup heavy whipping cream

Directions:

- Turn the Instant Pot on and press the "SAUTE" function key. Melt the butter.
- Add the onion and chicken. Cook for 10 minutes, until the chicken browned
- Stir in the green chiles, salt, cumin, oregano, black pepper, and frozen cauliflower
- Pour in the chicken broth. Cover and lock the instant pot, cooking on high pressure for 30 minutes
- Set aside for 10 minutes. Let the natural pressure release for 10 minutes

- Whisk in the sour cream and heavy whipping cream. Serve immediately.

Nutrition:

- Calories - 509
- Carbs - 12 g
- Carbs - 8.5 g
- Fat - 33 g
- Protein - 41g

CORIANDER SHREDDED CHICKEN

Serving: 2

Ingredients:

- 1 teaspoon coriander seeds
- ½ cup of water
- 1 teaspoon olive oil
- 1 teaspoon dried dill
- 1 teaspoon butter
- 1 teaspoon salt
- 7 oz chicken breast, skinless, boneless

Directions:

- Pour water in the crockpot.
- Add coriander seeds, dried dill, and salt.
- Cook the liquid for 1 hour on High.
- Meanwhile, preheat olive oil in the skillet and add chicken breast.
- Roast it for 2 minutes from each side.

- Then After this, with the help of the fork shred the chicken.
- Add butter and mix up well.
- Serve the shredded chicken with coriander gravy.

Nutrition:

- Calories - 151
- Fat - 6.7
- Carbs - 0.3
- Protein - 21.2

CHICKEN CHEESE RECIPE

Serving: 6

Ingredients:

- 6 boneless skinless chicken breasts
- 1 can (10 ounces condensed cream of chicken soup
- 1 can (10 ounces) condensed Fiesta cheese soup
- ⅛ teaspoon pepper
- 2 teaspoons chili powder
- Non-stick cooking spray

Directions:

- Grease a slow cooker and mix all of the ingredients in it.
- Cook everything on LOW for 6 to 8 hours.
- Make sure the chicken's internal temperature reaches 165°F.

Nutrition:

- Calories - 231
- Fat - 6 g
- Carbs - 20 g
- Protein - 23 g

CREAM CHEESE CHICKEN

Serving: 6

Ingredients:

- 1 lb chicken breasts, boneless and skinless
- 1 can (10 oz rotel tomato, undrained
- 1 can (15 oz) corn, undrained
- 1 can (15 oz) black beans, drained and rinsed
- 1 package (1 oz) dry ranch seasoning
- 1½ tsp chili powder
- 1½ tsp cu minutes
- 8 oz cream cheese
- ¼ cup parsley

Directions:

- Combine all of the ingredients, except cheese, in the Instant Pot.
- Close and lock the lid. Select MANUAL and cook at HIGH pressure for 20 minutes.
- When the timer goes off, let the pressure
- Release Naturally
- for 10 minutes, then release any remaining steam manually. Open the lid.

- Add the cheese to the pot and stir well. Close the lid a let sit for 5 minutes, until cheese is melted.
- Open the lid and return the chicken to the pot. Stir to combine.
- Top with parsley and serve.
- Notes: Serve with tortilla chips or rice.

CITRUS HERB CHICKEN CHORIZO

Serving: 6

Ingredients:

- 3 tablespoon grass-fed butter; ghee, or avocado oil
- 4 chicken thighs; bone-in
- 1 ¼ teaspoon sea salt
- 5 fresh thyme sprigs; leaves removed and stems discarded
- 1/2-pound chorizo; casing removed
- 1 medium yellow onion; sliced.
- 4 fresh garlic cloves; minced
- 1/3 cup sun-dried tomatoes
- 1/2 cup pitted green olives
- 1/3 cup freshly squeezed orange juice
- 3/4 cup chicken bone broth
- 1 handful fresh cilantro

Directions:

- Add 2 tablespoon grass-fed butter, ghee, or avocado oil to the Instant Pot and press "SAUTE" .*

- Add the chicken thighs, sprinkle with ½ teaspoon sea salt, and brown for about 2½ minutes per side. Remove the chicken and set aside.
- Add the remaining 1 tablespoon grass-fed butter, ghee, or avocado oil, onion, garlic, thyme, and the remaining ¾ teaspoon sea salt, sauteing for 5 minutes, stirring occasionally.
- Add the chorizo and saute for 5 minutes, stirring occasionally.
- Press the "KEEP WARM/CANCEL" button. Add the sun-dried tomatoes, olives, orange juice, and bone broth. Give it a good stir. Add the browned chicken, making sure it's submerged in liquid
- Cover the Instant Pot, making sure the steam release valve is sealed. Press the "POULTRY" setting, then increase the time using the *+* button until you reach 20 minutes.
- When the Instant Pot is done and beeps, press "KEEP WARM/CANCEL" * Quick release and open the steam release valve. Then carefully open the lid.
- Serve immediately, topped with fresh cilantro.

Nutrition:

- Calories - 769
- Carbs - 8 g
- Carbs - 5 g
- Fat - 50 g
- Protein - 47 g

ITALIAN BUFFALO CHICKEN

Serving: 2

Ingredients:

- 2 chicken breasts, boneless and skinless
- 1/2 cup buffalo wing sauce
- 1/2 cup Italian dressing

Directions:

- Put all ingredients in the crockpot. Mix thoroughly.
- Cook on low for 6 hours.

Nutrition:

- Calories - 287
- Fat - 17 g
- Carbs - 3 g
- Protein - 29 g
- Serving suggestions: Drizzle the sauce all over the chicken when serving.
- Tip: You can cook the recipe on high for 4 hours.

KNOCK OFF YOUR SOCKS CHICKEN AND SAUSAGE

Serving: 2

Ingredients:

- 2 chicken thighs, thawed
- 2 oz green chili
- 1 tsp garlic salt

Directions:

- Place chicken in the crockpot and cook for 6 hours on low.
- Drain the juices afterwards and add in the other two ingredients.
- Cover and cook for another 30 minutes on high.
- Shred chicken with a fork.

Nutrition:

- Calories - 336
- Fat - 21.9 g
- Carbs - 3 g
- Protein - 18.1 g
- Serving suggestions: Serve with tacos or in burritos.
- Tip: Instead of 8 hours, you can cook the chicken on high for 4 hours.

FLAVORED TURKEY WINGS

Serving: 4

Ingredients:

- 4 turkey wings
- 1 yellow onion, chopped
- 1 carrot, chopped
- 3 garlic cloves, minced
- 1 celery stalk, chopped
- 1 cup chicken stock
- Salt and black pepper to the taste
- 2 tablespoons olive oil
- A pinch of rosemary, dried
- 2 bay leaves
- A pinch of sage, dried
- A pinch of thyme, dried

Directions:

- In your slow cooker, mix turkey with onion, carrot, garlic, celery, stock, salt, pepper, oil, rosemary, sage, thyme and bay leaves, toss, cover and cook on Low for 8 hours.
- Divide between plates and serve hot.
- Enjoy!

Nutrition:

- Calories - 223
- Fat - 5
- Carbs - 18
- Protein - 14

INSTANT POT CHICKEN BIRYANI

Serving: 8

Ingredients:

- 2 teaspoon garam masala
- 1 tablespoon ginger paste
- 1 tablespoon garlic paste
- ½ teaspoon turmeric
- 1 tablespoon red chili powder
- ¼ cup cilantro, chopped
- ¼ cup mint leaves
- ¾ cup yogurt
- 2 tablespoons lemon juice
- 2 pounds whole chicken, cut into 12 pieces
- 3 tablespoons ghee
- 2 onions, sliced
- 1 jalapeno, chopped
- 3 cups basmati rice, soaked then rinsed
- Salt
- 3 cups water
- 1 teaspoon saffron + 1 tablespoon milk
- 6 hard-boiled eggs, peeled

Directions:

- Make the marinade by mixing in the bowl the garam masala, ginger paste, garlic paste, turmeric and red chili powder. Add the cilantro, mint, yogurt, and lemon juice. Marinate the chicken for at least 30 minutes in the fridge.
- While the chicken is marinating, press the Saute button on the Instant Pot. Add 1

- tablespoon of the ghee and saute the onions for 15 minutes until golden brown and caramelized. Set aside.
- Use another tablespoon of ghee and saute the jalapeno. Stir in the marinated chicken. Stir constantly for 3 minutes.
- Close the lid and seal the vent. Press the Manual button and adjust the cooking time to 5 minutes. Do quick pressure release.
- Once the lid is open, pour the rice over the chicken and add salt to taste and 3 cups of water. Stir in the saffron with milk.
- Close the lid and press the Manual button. Adjust the cooking time to 8 minutes.
- Do quick pressure release.
- Fluff the rice with the chicken and garnish with eggs and cooked onions. Sprinkle with chopped cilantro if desired.

Nutrition:

- Calories - 471
- Carbs - 65.1g
- Protein - 30.3
- Fat - 8.9g

CHICKEN SAUSAGE AND KALE SOUP

Serving: 6

Ingredients:

- 1 pound Chicken Sausage

- ½ cup Heavy Cream
- 2 cups chopped Kale
- 3 Garlic Cloves, minced
- 1 medium Cauliflower, broken into florets
- 5 cups Chicken Broth
- 1 tbsp. Red Pepper Flakes
- 1 tsp dried Fennel
- 1 Onion, chopped
- 2 tbsp. Olive Oil
- Salt and Pepper, to taste

Directions:

- Heat the oil in the IP on SAUTE.
- Add the onions and cook for 3 minutes.
- Add garlic, sausage, and fennel, and cook for about 5 minutes.
- Stir in the remaining ingredients, except kale and cream, and close the lid.
- Cook on MANUAL for 12 minutes.
- Release the pressure and stir in the kale and heavy cream.
- Season with salt and pepper and serve immediately.
- Enjoy!

Nutrition:

- Calories - 400
- Fat - 30g
- Carbs - 6g
- Protein - 22g

TURKEY CAULIFLOWER MEAL

Serving: 4

Ingredients:

- 1 cup cauliflower, chopped
- 1 teaspoon dried thyme, ground
- 1 pound turkey breasts
- 1 tablespoon fresh parsley, chopped (finely
- 1/2 teaspoon garlic powder

Directions:

- Make cauliflower puree in a blender.
- Take your Instant Pot and place over dry kitchen surface; open its top lid and switch it on.
- Add the 1 cup water, puree, garlic powder, and thyme in the cooking pot. Stir the ingredients to combine well.
- Close its top lid and make sure that its valve it closed to avoid spillage.
- Press "MANUAL" . Adjust the timer to 2 minutes.
- Pressure will slowly build up; let the added ingredients to cook until the timer indicates zero.
- Press "CANCEL". Now press "QPR" to quickly release pressure.
- Drain the cauliflower and add to a bowl. Cover and set aside.
- Empty the pot. Press "SAUTe". Grease the pot with some cooking oil.
- Add the turkey. Cook for 3-4 on each side.

- Add the cauliflower puree on top of the turkey cutlets. Serve.

Nutrition:

- Calories - 298
- Fat - 4g
- Carbs - 37g
- Sodium - 542mg
- Protein - 31g

SALMON FILLETS AND LEMON SAUCE

Serving: 4

Ingredients:

- 4 salmon fillets
- 2 tablespoons chili pepper
- Juice of 1 lemon
- 1 lemon, sliced
- 1 cup veggie stock
- 1 teaspoon sweet paprika
- 1 teaspoon basil, dried
- Salt and black pepper to the taste

Directions:

- In your slow cooker, mix chili pepper with lemon juice, stock, paprika, basil, salt and
- pepper and whisk.
- Add salmon fillets, top them with lemon slices, cover and cook on High for 2 hours.

- Divide salmon on plates, drizzle sauce from the Crockpot all over and serve.
- Enjoy!

Nutrition:

- Calories - 200
- Fat - 4
- Carbs - 16
- Protein - 3

SPICY TURKEY BREAST

Serving: 3

Ingredients:

- 10 oz turkey breast, skinless, boneless
- 1 teaspoon chili powder
- ½ teaspoon salt
- ½ teaspoon cayenne pepper
- ¾ cup of coconut milk
- ½ teaspoon dried oregano
- ¼ jalapeno pepper, minced
- 1 teaspoon butter
- ¼ cup crushed tomatoes

Directions:

- In the shallow bowl, mix up together chili powder, salt, cayenne pepper, and dried oregano.
- Rub the turkey breast with the spice mixture and Then add minced jalapeno pepper, crushed tomatoes, butter, and coconut milk.

- Close the lid and cook a turkey breast for 6 hours on Low.

Nutrition:

- Calories - 261
- Fat - 17.4
- Carbs - 9.9
- Protein - 18.2

SWEET TURKEY DRUMSTICKS

Serving: 5

Ingredients:

- ½ cup Water
- 6 Turkey Drumsticks
- ½ cup Soy Sauce
- 1 tsp Pepper
- 2 tsp Sweetener
- ½ tsp Garlic Powder
- 1 tsp Salt

Directions:

- Combine the spices in a small bowl.
- Rub the mixture into the turkey.
- Combine the water and soy sauce in the Instant Pot.
- Add the drumsticks and close the lid.
- Cook on MANUAL for 25 minutes.
- Release the pressure for 10 minutes.
- Serve and enjoy!

Nutrition:

- Calories - 209
- Fat - 15g
- Carbs - 3g
- Protein - 34g

TURKEY MINESTRONE

Serving: 8

Ingredients:

- 7 oz chicken thighs
- 1-pound turkey breast
- 7 cup water
- 6 oz diced tomatoes
- 1 teaspoon kosher salt
- 1 teaspoon ground black pepper
- ½ teaspoon paprika
- 1 teaspoon cilantro
- ½ teaspoon ground cu minutes
- 1 tablespoon garlic clove
- 1 oz bay leaf
- 6 oz pasta, cooked
- 3 oz Swiss chard
- 2 zucchinis
- 1/3 cup red kidney beans, cooked

Directions:

- Put the chicken thighs and turkey breast in the slow cooker bowl. Add the water and diced

onions. After this, add the kosher salt, ground black pepper, paprika, and cilantro.
- Then add the ground cumin and garlic cloves.
- Sprinkle the mixture with the bay leaf and cook on HIGH for 5 hours. When the time is done, remove the poultry from the slow cooker and shred well.
- Chop the zucchini and Swiss chard.
- Add the vegetables in the slow cooker. Then add the red kidney beans and shredded chicken and turkey. Close the lid and cook the dish for 3 hours on LOW.
- After this, add the cooked pasta and stir it carefully. Ladle the soup into the serving bowls and enjoy!

Nutrition:

- Calories - 173
- Fat - 6.6
- Carbs - 10.79
- Protein - 18

PORK, BEEF AND LAMB

STEAK AND BEANS

Serving: 6

Ingredients:

- 1 ½ pounds round steak
- 2 cups frozen corn, thawed and drained
- 1 14 ounce can black beans, rinsed and drained

- 1 18 ounce can of chunky garden salsa
- 1 medium onion, chopped
- ½ cup water
- ½ teaspoon salt
- Pinch or two of red pepper flakes

Directions:

- Combine all the ingredients, except beef, in a bowl and mix well.
- Trim the excess fat from the beef and cut it into 6 equal.
- Place the beef into the cooker and pour the mixture over it.
- Cover the lid and cook for 8 to 9 hours on LOW, or longer to reach desired tenderness.
- Serve hot.

Nutrition:

- Calories - 490
- Fat - 26.2 g
- Carbs - 34.2 g
- Protein - 28 g

WESTERN SHOULDER RIBS

Serving: 8

Ingredients:

- 3 pounds pork shoulder
- 2 teaspoons salt
- 1 teaspoon barbecue rub

- ½ cup water
- ½ cup commercial barbecue sauce

Directions:

- Place all ingredients in the Instant Pot.
- Close the lid and press the Meat/Stew button.
- Adjust the cooking time to 40 minutes.
- Do natural pressure release.

Nutrition:

- Calories - 470
- Carbs - 2.8g
- Protein - 43.7g
- Fat - 30.1g

CHUNKY AND BEANLESS BEEF CHILI

Serving: 6

Ingredients:

- 1 tablespoon oil
- 2 pounds beef chuck roast, cut into cubes
- Salt and pepper
- 1 tablespoon chili powder
- 2 tablespoons cumin powder
- 1 tablespoon paprika
- 1 cup beef broth
- 8 ounces Portobello mushrooms, chopped
- 1 tablespoon onion powder
- 1 can tomato paste

- 1 can crushed tomatoes

Directions:

- Press the Saute button on the Instant Pot.
- Heat the oil and saute the beef chuck roast until lightly golden on all sides.
- Season with salt and pepper to taste.
- Stir in the rest of the ingredients.
- Close the lid and press the Meat/Stew button.
- Adjust the cooking time to 60 minutes.
- Do natural pressure release.

Nutrition:

- Calories - 373
- Carbs - 15.4g
- Protein - 44.8g
- Fat - 15.8 g

BRAZILIAN BEEF STEW (FEIJOADA

Serving: 8

Ingredients:

- 4 tablespoons vegetable oil
- 1 onion, chopped
- 12 cloves of garlic, sliced
- 2 ½ pounds chuck stew meat
- Salt and pepper
- 2 poblano peppers, seeded and chopped
- 1 cup yellow squash, sliced

- 3 cups beef broth
- 1 cup tomatoes, chopped
- 2 tablespoons red wine vinegar
- 2 tablespoons chili powder
- 2 cans black beans, drained and rinsed

Directions:

- Press the Saute button on the Instant Pot.
- Heat the oil and saute the onion and garlic.
- Add in the beef stew meat and stir for another 3 minutes until lightly brown.
- Season with salt and pepper to taste.
- Stir in the rest of the ingredients.
- Close the lid and press the Meat/Stew button.
- Adjust the cooking time to 40 minutes.
- Do natural pressure release.
- Serve with rice and lime wedges.

Nutrition:

- Calories - 483
- Carbs - 24.4g
- Protein - 40.8g
- Fat - 24.4g

LAMB RIBLETS WITH HERBS

Serving: 4

Ingredients:

- 4 slabs of lamb riblets, about 2 lbs
- 3 garlic cloves, crushed

- 1 cup beef broth
- 1 tbsp lemon zest
- 4 tbsp olive oil
- ¼ cup shallots, chopped
- 4 tbsp butter
- 2 tsp capers
- Spices: ½ tsp sea salt
- 1 tsp dried oregano
- 1 tsp dried parsley
- 1 tsp fresh mint, finely chopped

Directions:

- Rinse the meat under cold running water and place on a clean work surface. Rub evenly with salt, oregano, and lemon zest. broth.
- Seal the lid and set the steam release handle to the "Sealing" position. Press the "MANUAL" button and cook for 20 minutes on high pressure.
- When done, release the pressure naturally for 10 minutes and then move the pressure valve to the "Venting" position to release any remaining pressure.
- Open the lid and remove the riblets from the pot. Press the "Saute" button and melt the butter.
- Add shallots and garlic. Cook for 3-4 minutes and then add the meat.
- Brown on both sides for 4-5 minutes.
- Remove from the pot and sprinkle with some fresh mint.
- Serve with capers.

Nutrition:

- Calories - 665
- Fat - 42.5g
- Carbs - 2.8g
- Protein - 65.5g

MEATY STUFFED PEPPERS

Serving: 4

Ingredients:

- 6 bell peppers, center cored (any color
- 1½ pounds ground beef
- 2-ounce can of black beans, drained and rinsed
- 3 cups Pepper Jack cheese, shredded
- 2 cups corn, drained
- 2 white onions, diced
- 3 diced tomatoes, chopped
- 8-ounce can of enchilada sauce
- ½ cup white wine
- 1 teaspoon cu minutes
- 1 teaspoon garlic powder
- Salt and black pepper, to taste
- 3 tablespoons olive oil

Directions:

Nutrition:

- Calories - 472
- Fat - 16.2 g
- Carbs - 25 g

- Protein - 53 g

ITALIAN BEEF SANDWICH FILLING

Serving: 6

Ingredients:

- 3 pounds chuck roast, cut into large chunks
- 1 envelope of dry Italian salad dressing (0.6-ounce
- 1 8-ounce jar pepperoncini pepper slices
- 1 8-ounce jar Giardiniera, drained (pickled vegetables)
- 1 14.5-ounce can beef broth

Directions:

- Place chuck roast in slow cooker.
- Add seasoning, pepperoncini peppers, Giardiniera, and beef broth.
- Make sure broth seeps under the meat as well.
- Cover and cook for 9 hours on LOW.
- Shred the meat and cook 1 hour longer on LOW.

Nutrition:

- Calories - 170
- Fat - 3.5 g
- Carbs - 1 g
- Protein - 13 g

- Note: for better results, trim the fat from the beef roast before cutting into chunks. Serve in hoagies buns with provolone cheese slices.

PULLED PORK WITH BBQ RUB

Serving: 4

Ingredients:

- Rub: 1 tablespoon brown sugar
- 1 teaspoon Black pepper Freshly ground.
- 2 teaspoon Ground ginger.
- 2 tablespoon Smoked paprika
- 2 teaspoon Cayenne pepper
- 1 tablespoon Dried oregano
- 1 tablespoon Garlic powder.
- 2 tablespoon Onion powder.
- 1 teaspoon Salt
- Pork: 2 kg Pork shoulder Cut into 5 or 6 chunks
- 3 tablespoon Tomato puree
- 1 tablespoon Olive oil
- 3 tablespoon White wine vinegar
- 1 tablespoon Honey
- 500 ml Water

Directions:

- Stir all of the rub ingredients together and rub all over your pieces of pork shoulder. If you have time, leave to absorb for 30 minutes-2 hours.
- Set the Instant Pot to "SAUTE" mode and heat the olive oil in it. Fry off the pork pieces in batches until golden brown all over.

- When all of the pork is browned and set to one side, keep the Instant Pot on "SAUTE" mode and use some of the water to scrape the meat bits off of the bottom of the pan as the water bubbles
- Pop the meat back in, leaving the meaty water at the bottom, add the vinegar, honey, tomato puree and the rest of the water
- Seal the lid of the Instant Pot and set the timer for 60 minutes.
- When the Instant Pot is finished, allow it to release the pressure naturally (will take about 15-25 minutes). Remove the pork to a bowl and switch on "SAUTE" mode again. Allow the sauce to reduce by half.
- Meanwhile shred or pull apart the pork into chunks. Add it back to the reduced sauce and stir well
- Check for seasoning and add more salt, pepper or honey if needed

Nutrition:

- Calories - 385
- Protein - 57g
- Fat - 15g
- Carbs - 5g

BEEF PICADILLO

Serving: 6

Ingredients:

- 12 oz lean ground beef

- 1/3 cup golden or dark raisins
- 14.5 oz unsalted diced tomatoes, undrained
- 1 bay leaf
- 1 onion, diced
- 1 tsp Sucanat
- 1 fresh jalapeno or Serrano pepper, minced
- 1/2 tsp ground cu minutes
- 1/2 tsp garlic powder
- 1/2 tsp ground nutmeg
- 3/4 tsp ground cinnamon
- 1/2 tsp crumbled dried thyme
- 1/4 tsp ground allspice
- 1/4 tsp sea salt
- 1/4 tsp freshly ground black pepper
- 10 oz frozen brown rice
- 1/4 cup dry roasted slivered almonds

Directions:

- Coat the slow cooker with nonstick cooking spray.
- Brown the beef in a nonstick skillet over medium high flame, then Add the bay leaves, tomatoes with their juices, raisins, onion, sugar, cinnamon, pepper, cumin, nutmeg, thyme, allspice, and garlic powder into the slow cooker.
- Cover and cook for 3 hours on high or for 6 hours on low.
- Prepare the rice based on manufacturer's instructions. Divide into separate.
- Remove the bay leaves from the slow cooker. Add the salt, pepper, and almonds. Divide the picadillo beef into equal portions on top of the rice. Serve warm.

Nutrition:

- Calories - 214

DOUBLE-SMOKED BACON AND LEEKS

Serving: 6

Ingredients:

- 6 double-smoked bacon slices, chopped
- 4 leeks, chopped
- 2 onions, chopped
- 2 jalapeno peppers, chopped
- 4 cloves garlic, minced
- 1 tablespoon fresh thyme, chopped
- 1 teaspoon ground cu minutes
- 2 teaspoons Cajun seasoning blend
- 1 cup white beans, drained and rinsed
- 1 cup chickpeas, drained and rinsed
- 1 can kidney beans, drained and rinsed
- 1 cup black beans, drained
- 4 teaspoons all-purpose flour
- 4 cups chicken broth
- 1 cup whipping cream
- 1 cup cheddar cheese, shredded

Directions:

- Press the SAUTe button of the Crock-Pot
- ®
- Express and let it preheat.

- Add bacon to the pot and cook until lightly brown.
- Drain the half of the bacon fat from the pot.
- Add onions and cook until brown.
- Add leeks, garlic, jalapeno, thyme, and cu minutes
- Stir well and season with Cajun seasoning blend.
- Let cook for 5 minutes.
- Add the white beans, black beans, chickpeas and kidney beans.
- Sprinkle the flour over the beans.
- Cook for a few minutes and then add the broth.
- Press the SLOW COOK button and let cook for 3 hours at low pressure. Make sure the steam valve is open.
- After 3 hours press the START/STOP button.
- Open the pot and add cream.
- Stir in cheese.
- Serve with bread.

Nutrition:

- Calories - 699
- Fat - 19.3 g
- Carbs - 95 g
- Protein - 39 g

BRATWURST STEW

Serving: 8

Ingredients:

- 1-pound bratwurst sausage links, chopped

- 1 jalapeno pepper, chopped
- 1 eggplant, chopped
- 1 tomato, chopped
- 1 garlic clove, peeled, crushed
- ½ cup snap peas
- 1 cup of water
- 1 tablespoon tomato paste
- ½ teaspoon salt
- 1 teaspoon smoked paprika
- 1 tablespoon butter

Directions:

- Put butter in the skillet and melt it.
- Add chopped eggplant and cook it for 4 minutes on the medium heat.
- Place the chopped sausages in the crockpot.
- Add jalapeno pepper, tomato, garlic clove, snap peas, tomato paste, salt, and smoked paprika.
- Then add roasted eggplants and water.
- Close the lid.
- Cook the stew for 6 hours on Low.
- Mix up the stew carefully before serving.

Nutrition:

- Calories - 226
- Fat - 18.2
- Carbs - 7.2
- Protein - 7.8

EASY BEEF AND BROCCOLI STIR FRY

Serving: 5

Ingredients:

- 1 tablespoon olive oil
- 1 onion, chopped
- 3 cloves of garlic, minced
- 1-pound flank steak, thinly sliced
- 1 tablespoon ginger, grated
- 1 tablespoon Shaoxing wine
- 2 tablespoons soy sauce
- ½ tablespoon oyster sauce
- 1/3 teaspoon five spice powder
- 1 cup beef broth
- ¼ teaspoon brown sugar
- 1 head broccoli, cut into florets
- 1 tablespoon cornstarch + 2 tablespoons water

Directions:

- Press the Saute button on the Instant Pot.
- Heat the oil and saute the onions and garlic until fragrant.
- Stir in the beef stew meat and stir for another 3 minutes until lightly brown.
- Add the rest of the ingredients except for the broccoli and cornstarch slurry.
- Close the lid and press the Meat/Stew button.
- Adjust the cooking time to 20 minutes.
- Do natural pressure release.

- Once the lid is open, press the Saute button and stir in the broccoli and cornstarch slurry.
- Allow simmering until the sauce thickens and the broccoli cooked.

Nutrition:

- Calories - 500
- Carbs - 55.4g
- Protein - 37.1g
- Fat - 15.4g

ROSEMARY BEEF

Serving: 2

Ingredients:

- 1 pound boneless chuck beef
- 2 teaspoons vegetable oil
- ¼ cup beef broth
- ¼ cup tomato sauce
- ¼ cup red wine
- 1 tablespoon Worcestershire sauce
- 2 tablespoons onion, minced
- 1 clove garlic, minced
- ½ teaspoon dried rosemary
- Salt and pepper to taste
- 1 teaspoon cornstarch
- Remove fat from meat. Place meat in slow cooker.
- In a medium bowl, combine chili beans in gravy, corn, tomatoes, green chilies, and chipotle pepper.

- Pour mixture over meat
- Cover and cook on LOW for 10-12 hours or on HIGH 5-6 hours.
- Mash potatoes for serving

Directions:

- In a medium skillet, heat the oil and brown the beef. In a mixing bowl, combine the other ingredients EXCEPT the cornstarch and water. Pour the sauce over the meat.
- Cover, and cook for 8 hours on LOW, until the meat is tender.
- Using a slotted spoon, Serve with mash potatoes

Nutrition:

- Calories - 354
- Fat - 19 g
- Carbs - 6 g
- Protein - 34 g

EASTERN MEAT LOAF

Serving: 8

Ingredients:

- 2 pounds ground beef
- 2 eggs
- 1 tablespoon sesame oil
- ¼ cup soy sauce
- ½ cup water chestnuts, chopped
- ½ cup scallions, chopped

- 1 cup zucchini, shredded
- 4 cups cabbage, shredded
- ½ cup beef stock

Directions:

- In a bowl, combine the ground beef, eggs, sesame oil, and soy sauce. Mix well.
- Next, add the water chestnuts, scallions, and zucchini. Mix well and form the meat into a loaf.
- Place the loaf in the center of a slow cooker.
- Surround the meat loaf with the shredded cabbage.
- Pour in the beef stock.
- Cover the slow cooker and cook on low for 8 hours.

Nutrition:

- Calories - 411.1
- Fat - 33.1 g
- Carbs - 5.8 g
- Protein - 21.9 g

TOMATO PORK CHOPS

Serving: 2

Ingredients:

- 2 pork chops, with bones
- 1 green bell pepper, sliced
- 1 cup cherry tomatoes
- 1 small onion, finely chopped.

- 4 tbsps. olive oil
- 1 cup beef broth
- ½ tsp. white pepper, freshly ground
- ¼ tsp. garlic powder
- ½ tsp salt

Directions:

- Place the meat in the pot and season with salt. Pour in the broth and seal the lid. Set the steam release handle to the "Sealing" position and press the "MANUAL" button.
- Set the timer for 15 minutes on high pressure. When done, release the pressure naturally and open the lid.
- Remove the meat from the pot and a
- deep bowl. Set aside
- Now press the "Saute" button and grease the inner pot with olive oil. Heat up and add onions and peppers. Sprinkle with some more salt. Cook for 5 - 6 minutes and then add cherry tomatoes. Pour in about 1/4 cup of the broth and simmer for 10 - 12 minutes, stirring occasionally.
- Season with pepper and garlic powder. Optionally, add some red pepper flakes. a
- food processor and process until smooth.
- Drizzle over pork chops and serve immediately.

Nutrition:

- Calories - 274
- Fat - 19.0g
- Protein - 24.0g
- Carbs - 9.0g

- Carbs - 8.0g
- Sugar - 2.0g

BRAISED PORK LOIN WITH PORT AND DRIED PLUMS

Serving: 10

Ingredients:

- 1 3¼-pound boneless pork loin roast, trimmed
- 1½ teaspoons freshly ground black pepper
- 1 teaspoon salt
- 1 teaspoon dry mustard
- 1 teaspoon dried sage (not rubbed sage
- ½ teaspoon dried thyme
- 1 tablespoon olive oil
- 2 cups onion, sliced
- 1 cup leek, finely chopped
- 1 cup carrot, diced
- ½ cup port wine (or any sweet red wine)
- ⅓ cup chicken broth
- 1 cup pitted dried plums
- 2 bay leaves
- 2 tablespoons cornstarch
- 2 tablespoons water

Directions:

Nutrition:

- Calories - 280
- Fat - 7.8 g
- Carbs - 17.7 g

- Protein - 32.2 g

PORK AND CABBAGES

Serving: 6-8

Ingredients:

- 4 lbs pork roast, cut into chunks
- 3 tbsp coconut oil
- 4 cloves garlic, minced
- 2 large onions, chopped
- 1 tsp kosher salt
- 1 cup water
- 1 head cabbage, chopped

Directions:

- Preheat the Instant Pot by selecting SAUTe. Add and heat the oil.
- Add the garlic and onions and saute for 5-6 minutes until the onion is Put the pork chunks in the pot and cook for 5 minutes on all sides.
- Season with salt and pepper and pour the water, stir well.
- Press the CANCEL key to stop the SAUTe function.
- Close and lock the lid. Select MANUAL and cook at HIGH pressure for 35 minutes.
- When the timer beeps, use aQuick Release. Carefully unlock the lid.
- Select SAUTe and add the cabbage, stir and bring to a simmer.
- Simmer the dish for 5 minutes.

- Serve.

LAMB SHANK WITH BURGUNDY

Serving: 2

Ingredients:

- 2 lamb shanks
- Salt and pepper to taste
- 1 tablespoon parsley
- 1 tablespoon garlic minced
- ¼ teaspoon dried oregano
- ¼ teaspoon lemon peel
- 2 teaspoons olive oil
- ¼ chopped onion
- ½ chopped carrot
- ½ cup Burgundy wine
- ½ teaspoon beef bouillon

Directions:

- Place the lamb in a 2-quart slow cooker and season it with salt, pepper, parsley, garlic, oregano, and lemon zest. Mix a little so the flavors can penetrate.
- Saute the onion with the carrot in a saucepan over medium heat for 3-6 minutes. Stir in the wine and the bouillon. Pour the mixture over the lamb.
- Cover, and cook for 8 hours, until the lamb is tender.
- Skim the fat from the juices, and serve them with the lamb.

Nutrition:

- Calories - 525
- Fat - 25 g
- Carbs - 5 g
- Protein - 54 g

EASY BEEF CHILI

Serving: 4-6

Ingredients:

- 1 lb ground beef
- ½ lb kidney beans, rinsed
- 1 can diced tomatoes
- ¼ cup tomato paste
- 1 medium white onion, diced
- 3 cloves garlic, chopped
- 1 green bell pepper, diced
- 7 cups beef broth
- 1 tsp salt
- ½ tsp ground black pepper

Directions:

- Combine all of the ingredients in the Instant Pot and stir to mix.
- Close and lock the lid. Select the BEAN/CHILI program and leave it on the default.
- Once cooking is complete, use a
- Natural Release
- for 10 minutes, then release any remaining pressure manually. Open the lid.

- Serve.

PULLED PORK

Serving: 12

Ingredients:

- ½ cup water
- 3 pounds pork shoulder, boneless
- For the rub
- 2 teaspoons paprika
- 1 teaspoon onion powder
- 1 teaspoon garlic powder
- 1 teaspoon kosher salt
- ½ teaspoon black pepper
- ½ teaspoon mustard powder
- 2 tablespoons apple cider vinegar

Directions:

- Pour the water into the slow cooker.
- Mix together all of the ingredients for the rub in a bowl and spread evenly over the pork.
- Lower into the slow cooker, being careful not to wash off the rub.
- Cook for 4 hours on HIGH. The meat should be tender and fall apart easily.
- If desired,

Nutrition:

- Calories - 265
- Fat - 16 g

- Carbs - 1 g
- Protein - 20 g

TERIYAKI PORK TENDERLOIN

Serving: 4

Ingredients:

- 2 pork tenderloins (1 lb each, cut into half
- 2 tbsp olive oil
- Salt and ground black pepper to taste
- 2 cups teriyaki sauce
- Sesame seeds, toasted
- 4 green onions, chopped

Directions:

- Set your instant pot on SAUTe mode, add the oil and heat it up.
- Rub all sides of the tenderloins with salt and pepper.
- Add the tenderloins and cook for few minutes until lightly brown on both sides. You may have to do it in two batches.
- Pour the teriyaki sauce over the meat. Close and lock the lid.
- Press the CANCEL button to reset the cooking program, then select the MANUAL setting and set the cooking time for 20 minutes at HIGH pressure.
- Once cooking is complete, select CANCEL and let
- Naturally Release

- for 10 minutes. Release any remaining steam manually. Uncover the pot.
- Slice the meat, top with toasted sesame seeds and green onions, serve.

BEEF CURRY

Serving: 4

Ingredients:

- 2 pounds beef steak, cubed
- 2 tablespoons olive oil
- 1 tablespoon mustard
- 2 and ½ tablespoons curry powder
- 2 yellow onions, chopped
- 2 garlic cloves, minced
- 10 ounces canned coconut milk
- 2 tablespoons tomato sauce
- Salt and black pepper to the taste

Directions:

- In your slow cooker, mix beef with oil, mustard, curry powder, onion, garlic, tomato paste, salt and pepper, stir, cover and cook on High for 3 hours and 40 minutes.
- Add coconut milk, stir, cook on High for 20 minutes more, divide into bowls and serve.
- Enjoy!

Nutrition:

- Calories - 400

- Fat - 18
- Carbs - 18
- Protein - 22

LAMB STEW

Serving: 4

Ingredients:

- 1 and ½ pounds lamb meat, cubed
- ¼ cup tapioca flour
- Black pepper to the taste
- A pinch of sea salt
- 2 tablespoons olive oil
- 1 teaspoon rosemary, dried
- 1 onion, sliced
- ½ teaspoon thyme, dried
- 2 cups water
- 1 cup baby carrots
- 2 cups sweet potatoes, chopped

Directions:

- In a bowl, mix lamb with tapioca and toss to coat.
- Heat up a pan with the oil over medium high heat, add meat, brown it on all sides and Heat up the pan again over medium high heat, add onion, stir, cook for 3 minutes and add to your slow cooker as well.
- Also add a pinch of salt, pepper, rosemary, thyme, water, carrots and sweet potatoes, stir, cover and cook on Low for 8 hours.

- Divide lamb stew between plates and serve hot.
- Enjoy!

Nutrition:

- Calories - 350
- Fat - 8
- Carbs - 6
- Protein - 16

ASIAN BEEF SHORT RIBS

Serving: 6-8

Ingredients:

- 12 beef short ribs
- 2 tbsp olive oil
- ½ tsp salt
- ½ cup soy sauce
- 1 cup tomato paste
- 2 tbsp apple cider vinegar
- 4 cloves garlic, minced
- ¼ cup ginger root, diced
- 2 tbsp sriracha sauce
- ¼ cup raw honey

Directions:

- Select the SAUTe setting on the Instant Pot and heat the oil.
- Season the ribs with salt. Add to the pot and cook for 5 minutes on each side, until browned.
- Brown the short ribs in batches.

- Add the soy sauce, tomato paste, apple cider, garlic, ginger, sriracha and honey to the pot.
- Stir the mixture well, at the same time, deglaze the pot by scraping the bottom to remove all of the brown bits.
- Return the ribs to the pot.
- Press the CANCEL key to stop the SAUTe function.
- Close and lock the lid. Select MANUAL and cook at HIGH pressure for 35 minutes.
- Once timer goes off, allow to
- Naturally Release
- for 10-15 minutes, then release any remaining pressure manually.
- Open the lid.
- Serve with the gravy.

SLOWLY COOKED LAMB SHOULDER KEBAB

Serving: 5

Ingredients:

- 2 lbs lamb shoulder, chopped into smaller pieces
- 1 cup tomatoes, chopped
- 2 celery stalks, chopped
- 1 onion, whole
- 1 garlic head, whole
- 3 tbsp olive oil
- 3 tbsp butter
- 1 cup Greek yogurt
- ¼ cup fresh parsley, finely chopped
- Spices: 1 tsp salt

- 1 tsp black pepper
- ½ tsp red chili flakes

Directions:

- Grease the bottom of the pot with olive oil. Add the meat along with tomatoes,
- celery stalks, onion, and garlic.
- Sprinkle with salt, pepper, and chili flakes.
- Pour in enough water to cover and seal the lid. Set the steam release handle to the "Sealing" position and press the "Slow Cook" button.
- Set the timer for 8 hours on low pressure.
- When done, release the pressure naturally and open the lid. Remove the meat from the pot and place on a large cutting board. Using a sharp cutting knife, chop into bite-sized pieces and set aside.
- Remove the liquid and vegetables from the pot and press the "Saute" button. Grease the inner pot with butter and add the meat.
- Cook for 5-6 minutes, stirring occasionally.
- Remove from the pot and chill for a while. Top with Greek yogurt and sprinkle with freshly chopped parsley.
- Serve immediately.

Nutrition:

- Calories - 527
- Fat - 29.6g
- Carbs - 6.2g
- Protein - 56.1g

BAJA PORK TACOS

Serving: 6

Ingredients:

- 1 ½ lb pork sirloin roast, halved
- 1 Tbsp reduced sodium taco seasoning
- 12 corn tortillas (6 inches each), warmed according to the instructions on the package
- ¾ cup shredded, part-skim mozzarella cheese
- 2 ½ cans (4 oz each) chopped green chilies
- 1 ½ tsp ground cu minutes
- 1 ½ cups shredded lettuce

Directions:

- Place pork roast in the slow cooker.
- Add chilies, cumin and taco seasoning into a bowl and spread all over the pork.
- Cover and cook for 7-8 hours on low or 3-4 hours on high or until cooked through.
- Remove pork with a slotted spoon and place on your cutting board. When cool enough to handle, shred the meat with a pair of forks.
- Carefully remove the fat floating on the top of the cooked liquid from the slow cooker. Discard the fat.
- Add shredded meat back into the slow cooker. Mix well.
- Cook for a few minutes until well heated.
- Spread tortillas on your countertop. Place lettuce and cheese on the tortillas.
- Top with shredded pork and serve.

Nutrition:

- Calories - 320 (2 tacos)

JUICY POT ROAST

Serving: 4

Ingredients:

- 1 Onion, sliced
- 2 tbsp. Coconut Oil
- 2 pounds Chuck Roast
- 2 cups Bone Broth
- Salt and Pepper, to taste

Directions:

- Melt the coconut oil in your IP on SAUTE.
- Season the meat with some salt and pepper.
- Place it in the pot and sear on all sides until browned.
- Pour the broth over and lock the lid.
- Cook on MANUAL for 70 minutes.
- Do a quick pressure release.
- Serve and enjoy!

Nutrition:

- Calories - 760
- Fat - 50g
- Carbs - 2.5g
- Protein - 67g

JAMAICAN JERK PORK

Serving: 4

Ingredients:

- 1 tbsp. Olive Oil
- 2 pounds Pork Shoulder
- 1 cup Beef Broth
- 2 tbsp. Jamaican Spice Rub

Directions:

- Heat the oil in your IP on SAUTE.
- Add pork and cook on all sides, until browned.
- Combine the spices and broth and pour over.
- Close the lid and cook on MANUAL for 45 minutes.
- Release the pressure quickly.
- Shred the meat with forks inside the pot.
- Serve and enjoy!

Nutrition:

- Calories - 720
- Fat - 58g
- Carbs - 1.7g
- Protein - 55g

CHEESY MEAT PASTA

Serving: 2

Ingredients:

- 4 ounces mozzarella cheese
- 1 cup pasta sauce
- 1 cup water
- ¼ pound ground beef
- ¼ pound ground pork
- 6 ounces ruffles pasta
- 4 ounces ricotta cheese
- Cooking oil

Directions:

- Switch on the pot after placing it on a clean and dry platform. Press "Saute" cooking function.
- Open the pot lid; add the oil, pork, and beef in the pot; cook for 3-4 minutes to cook well and evenly browned.
- Mix the water, pasta, and sauce.
- Close the pot by closing the top lid. Also, ensure to seal the valve.
- Press "MANUAL" cooking function and set cooking time to 5 minutes. It will start cooking after a few minutes. Let the pot mix cook under pressure until the timer reads zero.
- Press "Cancel" cooking function and press "Quick release" setting.
- Open the pot, mix the cheese and serve warm. Enjoy it with your loved one!

Nutrition:

- Calories - 588
- Fat - 24g
- Carbs - 52.5g
- Protein - 61g

SNACKS AND APPETIZERS

SPICY SAUSAGE APPETIZER

Serving: 12

Ingredients:

- 2 pounds spicy pork sausage, sliced
- 18 ounces Paleo apple jelly
- 9 ounces mustard

Directions:

- In your slow cooker, mix apple jelly with mustard and whisk really well.
- Add spicy sausage slices, toss really well, cover and cook on Low for 2 hours.
- Divide sausage slices between bowls and serve them as an appetizer.
- Enjoy!

Nutrition:

- Calories - 231

- Fat - 4
- Carbs - 7
- Protein - 5

INCREDIBLE SPINACH DIP

Serving: 4

Ingredients:

- 1 cup almond milk
- 1 cup cashews, soaked for 2 hours and drained
- 2 tablespoons lemon juice
- 2 garlic cloves, chopped
- 2 teaspoons mustard
- 28 ounces canned artichokes, drained and chopped
- 8 ounces spinach
- 8 ounces canned water chestnuts, drained
- Black pepper to the taste
- Avocado mayonnaise

Directions:

- 1 cup coconut sugar
- 1 and ½ tablespoon cinnamon powder
- 1 egg white
- 2 teaspoons vanilla extract
- 4 cups pecans
- ¼ cup water
- Cooking spray
- In your food processor, mix cashews with garlic, almond milk, mustard and lemon juice and blend well.

- Stir, cover and cook on High for 2 hours.
- Leave your dip to cool down, add avocado mayo, stir well, divide into bowls and serve.
- Enjoy!

Nutrition:

- Calories - 200
- Fat - 4
- Carbs - 8
- Protein - 5

SAUSAGE DIP

Serving: 8

Ingredients:

- 8 oz sausage, cooked
- 4 tablespoons sour cream
- 2 tablespoons Tabasco sauce
- ½ cup cream cheese
- 3 tablespoons chives
- 5 oz salsa
- 4 oz Monterey Cheese

Directions:

- Chop the sausages and combine with the sour cream.
- Add chives and salsa. Chop Monterey cheese and add it to the slow cooker.
- Stir it gently and close the slow cooker lid. Cook the dish on LOW for 5 hours.

- Stir the dip every 30 minutes.
- When the sausage dip is cooked,

Nutrition:

- Calories - 184
- Fat - 14.4
- Carbs - 5.11
- Protein - 10

SLOW COOKER CHEESE DIP

Serving: 8

Ingredients:

- 2-pound Velveeta cheese
- 7 oz ground beef
- 1 red onion, chopped
- 1 chili pepper
- ½ cup water
- 1 tablespoon taco seasoning
- 1 teaspoon salt
- 1 tablespoon olive oil
- 1 tablespoon dried dill

Directions:

- Put the olive oil in the skillet. Add the chopped onion, ground beef, salt, dried dill, and taco seasoning.
- Chop the chili pepper and add it to the meat mixture too.

- Close the lid and cook the meat mixture for 10 minutes or until is it totally cooked.
- Put the meat mixture in the slow cooker. Add water and Velveeta cheese.
- Stir gently. Close the slow cooker lid and cook the dish on HIGH for 2 hours.
- When the cheese is melted, stir it gently again.
- Serve it.

Nutrition:

- Calories - 363
- Fat - 21.3
- Carbs - 16.28
- Protein - 26

CAULIFLOWER DIP

Serving: 6

Ingredients:

- 1 yellow onion, chopped
- 2 garlic cloves, minced
- 4 cups cauliflower florets, chopped
- 12 ounces coconut cream
- 1 tablespoon chopped scallions
- ½ cup avocado mayonnaise
- A pinch of salt and black pepper

Directions:

- In your slow cooker, combine all the ingredients, cover and cook on low for 4 hours.

- Blend using an immersion blender, divide into bowls and serve as a party dip.

Nutrition:

- Calories - 240
- Fat - 23,6
- Carbs - 8,8
- Protein - 2,9

TENDER ALMOND SHRIMPS

Serving: 4

Ingredients:

- 1 tablespoon almond flakes
- 1 tablespoon almond flour
- 1 oz Parmesan, grated
- ¾ teaspoon cayenne pepper
- 1 tablespoon butter
- ½ cup organic almond milk
- 9 oz shrimps, peeled

Directions:

- Mix up together almond flakes, almond flour, and Parmesan.
- Sprinkle the shrimps with cayenne pepper and place in the crockpot.
- Add almond milk.
- Cook the shrimp for 1.5 hours on High.
- Then open the lid and top the shrimps with Parmesan mixture.

- Close the lid and cook appetizer for 30 minutes on High.

Nutrition:

- Calories - 184
- Fat - 10.7
- Carbs - 3.3
- Protein - 19

KIDS FAVORITE PECANS

Serving: 30

Ingredients:

- For Pecans: 1 tsp butter
- 4 cups raw pecans
- ¼ cup Erythritol
- ½ tsp ground cinnamon
- Pinch of sea salt
- ½ cup filtered water
- For Chocolate coating: 2 tbsp. Erythritol
- 1 tsp ground cinnamon
- 1 (
- 20-ounce) block 85% dark chocolate

Directions:

- Place the butter in the Instant Pot and select "Saute". Then, add all ingredients except water and cook for about 5 minutes, stirring frequently.
- Select the "Cancel" and stir in water.

- Secure the lid and place the pressure valve to "Seal" position.
- Select "MANUAL" and cook under "High Pressure" for about 10 minutes.
- Meanwhile, preheat the oven to 350 degrees F.
- Select the "Cancel" and carefully do a "Natural" release for about 10 minutes and then do a "Quick" release.
- Remove the lid and Bake for about 5 minutes.
- Remove from oven and keep aside to cool.
- For coating: dust the pecans with the Erythritol and cinnamon.
- In a heatproof bowl, place chocolate.
- In the bottom of Instant Pot, arrange a steamer trivet and pour 1 cup of water.
- Place the bowl on top of trivet and select "Saute". Cook for about 5-6 minutes or until melted completely.
- Select the "Cancel" and Add pecans and coat well.
- Remove from bowl and keep aside to cool completely before serving.

Nutrition:

- Calories - 129
- Fat - 8.3g
- Carbs - 0.46g
- Protein - 1.7g

ARTICHOKE SPREAD

Serving: 8

Ingredients:

- 3 cups artichoke hearts, peeled and chopped
- 4 garlic cloves, minced
- 5 ounces coconut cream
- ½ teaspoon garlic powder
- ¼ teaspoon onion powder
- ¼ teaspoon sweet paprika
- 2 teaspoons olive oil
- ½ cup vegetable stock

Directions:

- In your slow cooker, combine all the ingredients, cover and cook on low for 3 hours.
- Stir well, divide into bowls and serve as a party spread

Nutrition:

- Calories - 77
- Fat - 5,5
- Carbs - 5,6
- Protein - 1,8

THREE-CHEESE SPAGHETTI SQUASH

Serving: 2

Ingredients:

- 1/2 large spaghetti squash
- 1 tbsp butter
- 1/4 oz Asiago cheese, grated
- 1/4 oz Parmesan cheese, grated
- 1/8 cup mozzarella, shredded

Directions:

- Cook the spaghetti squash in the crockpot for 6 hours on low.
- When cooked, remove the squash from the crockpot, discard the seeds and scoop out the insides of the squash and put it back inside the crockpot with butter and some garlic.
- Add the cheese in the crockpot, with mozzarella on top.
- Cover and cook for 30 minutes on high.

Nutrition:

- Calories - 192
- Fat - 14 g
- Carbs - 6.4 g
- Protein - 8.3 g
- Serving suggestions: Garnish with fresh basil.

SHIITAKE MUSHROOM BITES

Serving: 10

Ingredients:

- 7 oz shiitake mushroom
- 2 eggs
- 1 tablespoon cream cheese
- 3 tablespoons panko bread crumbs
- 2 tablespoons flour
- 1 teaspoon minced garlic
- 1 teaspoon salt
- ½ teaspoon chili flakes
- 1 teaspoon olive oil
- 1 teaspoon ground coriander
- ½ teaspoon nutmeg
- 1 tablespoon almond flour
- 1 teaspoon butter

Directions:

- Chop the shiitake mushrooms and put them in a skillet.
- Sprinkle the mushrooms with the salt, minced garlic, chili flakes, olive oil, ground coriander, and nutmeg. Roast the shiitake mushrooms for 5 minutes over medium heat.
- Beat the eggs in a bowl then add cream cheese, flour and bread crumbs. Add the shiitake mushroom mixture and butter.
- Knead into a smooth dough. Add more flour if the dough is sticky.

- Make the medium bites from the shiitake mushroom dough. Close the lid and cook the shiitake mushroom bites for 3 hours on HIGH.
- Turn the bites over and cook for 2 hours more on HIGH. Dry the mushroom bites with a paper towel if desired. Enjoy!

Nutrition:

- Calories - 65
- Fat - 3.5
- Carbs - 6.01
- Protein - 3

BANANA BREAD

Serving: 6

Ingredients:

- 10 oz biscuit mix
- 4 eggs
- 1 teaspoon vanilla extract
- 1 tablespoon sugar
- 12 oz banana, ripe
- 1/3 cup butter
- 1 teaspoon brown sugar

Directions:

- Beat the eggs in the mixing bowl. Melt butter and add it into the whisked eggs.
- Add vanilla extract, sugar, and brown sugar. Peel the bananas and mash them with a fork.

- Add the mashed bananas into the egg mixture.
- Mix and add the biscuit mix. Blend until smooth. After this, cover the slow cooker bowl with parchment and pour the batter inside.
- Close the slow cooker lid and cook the banana bread for 4 hours on HIGH.
- When the time is over, check if the banana bread is cooked with a toothpick. Remove the bread from the slow cooker and let cool.
- Slice and enjoy!

Nutrition:

- Calories - 506
- Fat - 20.2
- Carbs - 75.31
- Protein - 11

SMOKIES

Serving: 6

Ingredients:

- 1-pound smokies sausages
- ½ oz dark chocolate
- ½ cup tomato sauce
- 1 teaspoon butter
- 1 teaspoon chili powder
- ½ teaspoon minced garlic

Directions:

- Put smokie sausages, dark chocolate, tomato sauce, butter, chili powder, and mixed garlic in the crockpot.
- Mix up the ingredients with the help of the spatula.
- Close the lid and cook a snack for 2.5 hours on Low.
- Shake the cooked smokies well and

Nutrition:

- Calories - 267
- Fat - 22.9
- Carbs - 5.5
- Protein - 9.9

SLOW COOKER MEATBALLS WITH SESAME SEEDS

Serving: 9

Ingredients:

- 3 tablespoons milk
- 5 tablespoons panko bread crumbs
- 1 egg
- 3 tablespoons dried parsley
- 1 teaspoon minced garlic
- 1 teaspoon salt
- 14 oz ground pork
- 1 tablespoon sesame seeds
- ½ cup tomato paste

- 1 onion
- 1 tablespoon sugar
- 1 teaspoon cilantro
- 1 teaspoon cayenne pepper

Directions:

- Combine the ground pork and beaten egg together. Add the dried parsley, salt, minced garlic, panko bread crumbs, sesame seeds, and milk.
- Mix the ground pork mixture with your hands. Form the small meatballs and put the meatballs into the freezer.
- Meanwhile, combine the tomato paste, sugar, cilantro, and cayenne pepper together.
- Peel the onion and grate it then add the grated onion into the tomato paste mixture and stir it.
- Place the tomato paste in the slow cooker bowl.
- Add the frozen meatballs and close the slow cooker lid.
- Cook the dish for 9 hours on LOW. When the meatballs are cooked, let them cool briefly and serve.
- Enjoy!

Nutrition:

- Calories - 142
- Fat - 5.3
- Carbs - 8.26
- Protein - 16

RADISH LEMON SNACK

Serving: 2

Ingredients:

- 1 tbs. chives, chopped
- ½ cup water
- 2 cups radishes, make quarters
- 1 tbs. lemon zest
- A pinch of salt and pepper
- 2 tbs. olive oil

Directions:

- In a mixing bowl, combine the radishes with salt, pepper, chives, lemon zest and oil and toss to coat.
- Switch on your instant pot after placing it on a clean and dry kitchen platform.
- Pour the water into the cooking pot area. Arrange the trivet inside it; arrange the radishes over the trivet.
- Close the pot by closing the top lid. Also, ensure to seal the valve.
- Press "MANUAL" cooking function and set cooking time to 12 minutes. It will start cooking after a few minutes. Let the pot mix cook under pressure until the timer reads zero.
- Turn off and press "Cancel" cooking function. Quick release pressure.
- Open the pot and serve on a serving plate or bowl. Enjoy the Paleo dish!

Nutrition:

- Calories - 124
- Fat - 12g
- Carbs - 3.5g
- Protein - 13.5g

TRADITIONAL BRITISH SCOTCH EGGS

Serving: 4

Ingredients:

- 4 large organic eggs
- 1 pound gluten-free country style ground sausage
- 1 tbsp. olive oil

Directions:

- In the bottom of Instant Pot, arrange a steamer basket and pour 1 cup of water.
- Place eggs into the steamer basket.
- Secure the lid and place the pressure valve to "Seal" position.
- Select "MANUAL" and cook under "High Pressure" for about 6 minutes.
- Select the "Cancel" and carefully do a Quick release.
- Remove the lid and After cooling, peel the eggs.
- Divide sausage into 4 equal sized portions.
- Flat each portion into an oval-shaped patty.
- Place 1 egg in the middle of each patty and gently, mold the meat around the egg.

- Remove the basket from Instant Pot and drain the water.
- Place the oil in the Instant Pot and select "Saute". Then add the scotch eggs and garlic and cook until golden brown from all sides.
- Arrange a steamer trivet in the bottom of Instant Pot. Add 1 cup of water in Instant Pot.
- Place the scotch eggs on top of the trivet.
- Secure the lid and place the pressure valve to "Seal" position.
- Select "MANUAL" and cook under "High Pressure" for about 6 minutes.
- Select the "Cancel" and carefully do a Quick release.
- Remove the lid and serve immediately.

Nutrition:

- Calories - 486
- Fat - 40.6g
- Carbs - 0.1g
- Protein - 28.3g

BROCCOLI BITES

Serving: 2

Ingredients:

- 1 broccoli head, florets separated
- A pinch of salt and black pepper
- 2 tablespoons chicken stock
- 1 tablespoon chives, chopped
- ½ teaspoon garlic powder

- 2 tablespoons olive oil

Directions:

- In your slow cooker, combine all the ingredients, cover and cook on low for 4 hours.
- Divide into bowls and serve cold.

Nutrition:

- Calories - 185
- Fat - 14,7
- Carbs - 12,7
- Protein - 5,3

POOL-PARTY MEATBALLS

Serving: 8

Ingredients:

- 1½ pounds grass-fed ground beef
- ½ cup finely chopped bacon
- ½ cup almond flour
- 1 tsp garlic powder
- ½ tsp parsley flakes
- Salt and freshly ground black pepper, to taste
- 1½ cups sugar-free ketchup
- ½ cup sugar-free steak sauce
- 2 cups filtered water
- ¼ cup shredded Parmesan cheese

Directions:

- In a large bowl, add

- all ingredients except ketchup, steak sauce, water and cheese and mix until well combined.
- Make equal sized meatballs from the mixture.
- In another bowl, add ketchup, steak sauce and water and mix well.
- In the bottom of Instant Pot, place meatballs and top with ketchup mixture.
- Secure the lid and place the pressure valve to "Seal" position.
- Select "MANUAL" and cook under "High Pressure" for about 5 minutes.
- Select the "Cancel" and carefully do a Quick release.
- Remove the lid and immediately, sprinkle with cheese.
- Serve immediately.

Nutrition:

- Calories - 223
- Fat - 9.9g
- Carbs - 1.42g
- Protein - 22.4g

SOUTHERN BOILED PEANUTS

Serving: 6

Ingredients:

- 1 pound jumbo raw peanuts
- ½ cup sea salt
- 1 tbsp. Cajun seasoning
- Filtered water, as required

Directions:

- Rinse the peanuts under cold running water and remove any twigs and roots.
- In the bottom of Instant Pot, place peanuts, salt, Cajun seasoning and enough water to cover the peanuts and stir.
- Place a plate or trivet on top of peanuts.
- Secure the lid and place the pressure valve to "Seal" position.
- Select "MANUAL" and cook under "High Pressure" for about 65-90 minutes.
- Select the "Cancel" and carefully do a "Natural" release.
- Remove the lid and keep aside to cool.
- Drain well and serve.

Nutrition:

- Calories - 429
- Fat - 37.2g
- Carbs - 2.03g
- Protein - 19.5g

SHRIMP BOIL

Serving: 4

Ingredients:

- 8 king shrimps, peeled
- ½ cup of water
- ½ teaspoon ground coriander
- ½ teaspoon ground paprika

- ½ teaspoon salt
- 1 tablespoon butter
- ¼ cup snap peas

Directions:

- Put shrimps and snap peas in the crockpot.
- Add water, ground coriander, paprika, salt, and butter.
- After this, close the crockpot lid.
- Cook the shrimp boil for 3.5 hours on High.

Nutrition:

- Calories - 36
- Fat - 3
- Carbs - 1.5
- Protein - 1

DESSERTS

PARSLEY DIP WITH BLUE CHEESE

Serving: 7

Ingredients:

- 1 cup parsley
- 8 oz celery stalk
- 6 oz Blue cheese
- 1 tablespoon apple cider vinegar
- 6 oz cream

- 1 teaspoon minced garlic
- 1 teaspoon paprika
- ¼ teaspoon ground red pepper
- 1 onion

Directions:

- Chop the fresh parsley and celery stalk.
- Then chop blue cheese and add to the parsley and celery. Whip the cream and add it to the cheese mixture. Place in the slow cooker bowl.
- Sprinkle the parsley mixture with the minced garlic, paprika, ground red pepper, and apple cider vinegar. Peel the onion and grate it.
- Add the grated onion in the slow cooker and close the lid.
- Cook on LOW and cook for 7 hours.
- Mix the dip up with the help of the wooden spoon after 4 hours of the cooking. After the dish is cooked, remove it from the slow cooker and chill lightly. Stir the dip one more time. Enjoy!

Nutrition:

- Calories - 151
- Fat - 11.9
- Carbs - 5.14
- Protein - 7

NUTELLA GRANOLA

Serving: 6

Ingredients:

- 2 tablespoons Nutella
- 2 tablespoons honey
- 1 tablespoon raisins
- 1 cup granola
- 5 tablespoons pumpkin puree
- 1 teaspoon cinnamon
- ½ teaspoon ground ginger
- 1 teaspoon ground cardamom
- 3 tablespoons olive oil
- 3 tablespoons sunflower seeds

Directions:

- Place the granola in the slow cooker.
- Add raisins, pumpkin puree, cinnamon, ground ginger, ground cardamom, and sunflower seeds. Mix well and close the slow cooker lid.
- Cook the mixture on LOW for 3 hours. Meanwhile, combine Nutella, honey, and olive oil together.
- Mix well. When the time is done, pour the honey mixture into the slow cooker and stir it carefully.
- After this, close the slow cooker lid and cook the dish for 30 minutes on LOW. Then Mix it well. Cool the mixture well and separate it into 6. Enjoy!

Nutrition:

- Calories - 372
- Fat - 25.1
- Carbs - 32.2
- Protein - 6

ROSEMARY FINGERLING POTATOES

Serving: 15

Ingredients:

- 2 lb. fingerling potatoes
- 8 oz bacon
- 1 teaspoon onion powder
- 1 teaspoon chili powder
- 1 teaspoon garlic powder
- 1 teaspoon paprika
- 3 tablespoons butter
- 1 teaspoon dried dill
- 1 tablespoon rosemary

Directions:

- Wash the fingerling potatoes carefully.
- Butter the slow cooker bowl and make a layer of fingerling potatoes there.
- Combine the onion powder, chili powder, garlic powder, paprika, and dried dill together in a separate bowl.
- Stir lightly. Sprinkle the layer of fingerling potatoes with the spice mixture.

- Then slice the bacon and combine it with the rosemary.
- Cover the fingerling potatoes with the sliced bacon and close the slow cooker lid. Cook the dish on LOW for 8 hours. Serve the snack immediately. Enjoy!

Nutrition:

- Calories - 117
- Fat - 6.9
- Carbs - 12.07
- Protein - 3

CHARLOTTE

Serving: 8

Ingredients:

- 6 eggs
- 1 cup flour
- 1 cup apples
- 1 cup sugar
- 1 cup flour
- 1 teaspoon vanilla extract
- 1 teaspoon butter
- 1 teaspoon powdered sugar
- 1 pinch fresh minutes

Directions:

- Separate the egg whites and egg yolks. Start to whisk the egg yolks.

- When the egg yolks are fluffy, add the sugar and continue to whisk it until you get a bright yellow color. Add the vanilla extract.
- Then whisk the egg whites carefully until you get stiff peaks.
- Add the flour and stir it gently with a silicone spatula. Then combine the egg yolk mixture and the egg white mixture together.
- Stir it carefully. Slice the apples. Butter the slow cooker bowl and pour the batter
- inside. After this, add the sliced apples and close the lid.
- Cook the Charlotte for 5 hours on LOW.
- Check if the Charlotte is cooked and remove it from the slow cooker. Chill it well. The Charlotte may deflate as it cools. Cut into pieces and sprinkle with the powdered sugar and fresh mint. Enjoy!

Nutrition:

- Calories - 296
- Fat - 8.7
- Carbs - 43.51
- Protein - 10

ALMOND STRAWBERRY SQUARES

Serving: 8

Ingredients:

- 1 ½ cup almond flour

- ¼ cup almonds, ground
- 1 tbsp. cocoa powder, unsweetened
- 1 tsp baking powder
- ½ cup heavy cream
- ½ cup almond milk
- 1 large egg
- 1 tsp vanilla extract
- For the strawberry layer: ½ cup fresh strawberries, chopped
- 1 cup whipped cream
- 2 tbsp. Greek yogurt

Directions:

- In a large mixing bowl, combine almond flour, ground almonds, and cocoa powder.
- Mix until well combined
- In a separate bowl, whisk eggs, heavy cream, and vanilla extract. Now, combine dry and wet ingredients and mix together until well incorporated.
- Plug in your instant pot and pour in 2 cups of water. Position a trivet in the stainless steel insert. Line a 6-inches springform pan with some parchment paper. Spread the previously prepared mixture evenly and place the pan on top of a trivet. Securely lock the lid and adjust the steam release handle. Press the "MANUAL" button and set the timer for 8 minutes.
- Cook on high pressure.
- When done, perform a quick release and open the pot. Carefully Meanwhile, combine all strawberry layer ingredients in a food processor. Pulse until creamy. Spoon this mixture onto

chilled crust. Using a kitchen spatula, spread the mixture evenly.
- Refrigerate for 45 minutes, or freeze for 20 minutes. Cut into squares before serving.

Nutrition:

- Calories - 171
- Fat - 15.8g
- Carbs - 3.2g
- Protein - 3.9g

PORK CHEESE ROLLS

Serving: 8

Ingredients:

- 3 oz Monterey cheese, sliced
- 6 oz ground pork
- 2 oz onion, chopped
- 1 tablespoon sliced garlic
- 1 teaspoon salt
- 1 teaspoon ground pepper
- 5 oz Cheddar cheese, sliced
- 1 tablespoon pesto sauce
- 8 flour tortilla
- 1 teaspoon olive oil

Directions:

- Pour the olive oil in the slow cooker.

- Add ground pepper, pesto sauce, chopped onion, and ground pork. Close the slow cooker lid and cook the meat on HIGH for 5 hours.
- When the ground meat is cooked, place it on the flour tortillas.
- Sprinkle every flour tortilla with the chopped cheese.
- Roll the flour tortillas and put them in the slow cooker. There should be remaining oil from the ground meat in the slow cooker.
- Close the lid and cook on HIGH for 2 hours.
- When the time is done, check if the cheese in the tortillas is melted. Remove the cheese rolls from the slow cooker and cut them into 2 parts. Serve the snack!

Nutrition:

- Calories - 270
- Fat - 10.8
- Carbs - 27.52
- Protein - 16

SPICY SAUSAGE APPETIZER

Serving: 12

Ingredients:

- 2 pounds spicy pork sausage, sliced
- 18 ounces Paleo apple jelly
- 9 ounces mustard

Directions:

- In your slow cooker, mix apple jelly with mustard and whisk really well.
- Add spicy sausage slices, toss really well, cover and cook on Low for 2 hours.
- Divide sausage slices between bowls and serve them as an appetizer.
- Enjoy!

Nutrition:

- Calories - 231
- Fat - 4
- Carbs - 7
- Protein - 5

PEANUT CHICKEN STRIPS

Serving: 7

Ingredients:

- 3 tablespoons peanut butter, melted
- 1-pound chicken breast, boneless, skinless
- 1 teaspoon paprika
- 1 teaspoon salt
- 1 teaspoon olive oil
- 2 tablespoons almond flour
- 1 teaspoon cayenne pepper

Directions:

- Cut the chicken breast into the thick strips.

- Then sprinkle the chicken strips with the paprika, salt, and cayenne pepper.
- Coat the chicken strips in the almond flour. Pour the olive oil into the slow cooker and add the coated chicken strips.
- Close the slow cooker lid and cook the chicken strips for 4 hours on HIGH. Open the slow cooker lid and stir the chicken strips carefully.
- Close the lid and cook the snack for 2 hours more on LOW. Chill the chicken strips very well. Serve!

Nutrition:

- Calories - 161
- Fat - 9.5
- Carbs - 3.15
- Protein - 16

KETO MOCHA DE CREME

Serving: 4

Ingredients:

- 2 large eggs; separated
- 3 tablespoon brewed espresso
- 3 tablespoon stevia powder
- 1 cup coconut milk; full-fat
- 3/4 cup heavy cream
- 2 tablespoon cocoa powder; unsweetened.
- 1 teaspoon vanilla extract
- 1/4 teaspoon salt

Directions:

- In a small bowl, whisk together eggs, cocoa powder, espresso, stevia powder, vanilla, and salt, Set aside.
- Plug in the instant pot and press the "SAUTE" button. Pour in the coconut milk and heavy cream. Give it a good stir and warm up.
- Press the "CANCEL" button and slowly pour the warm milk mixture over the egg mixture, whisking constantly
- Divide the mixture between 4 ramekins and loosely cover with aluminum foil.
- Position a trivet at the bottom of your pot and pour in 2 cups of water. Gently place the ramekins on top and seal the lid.
- Set the steam release handle to the "SEALING" position and press the "MANUAL" button.
- Cook for 15 minutes
- When done; perform a quick pressure release and open the lid. Remove the ramekins and a
- room temperature and then refrigerate for about an hour

Nutrition:

- Calories - 257
- Fat - 25.5g
- Carbs - 3.5g
- Protein - 5.5g

ALMOND AND CHOCOLATE CANDY

Serving: 4-6

Ingredients:

- 14 oz condensed coconut milk
- 12 oz dark chocolate chips
- 2 cups water
- 1 cup almonds, chopped

Directions:

- In a baking pan that can fit into the pot, combine the chocolate chips and coconut milk.
- Cover the pan tightly with aluminum foil.
- Pour the water into the Instant Pot and set a steam rack in the pot.
- Place the pan on the rack. Close and lock the lid.
- Select MANUAL and cook at HIGH pressure for 3 minutes.
- When time is up, do aQuick Release. Carefully unlock the lid.
- Add the almonds and mix well.
- Line a sheet pan with a parchment paper. With a tablespoon, drop the candy onto the paper.
- Slip the pan into the freezer for about 10-20 minutes. Serve.

FISH STICKS

Serving: 4

Ingredients:

- 2 eggs, whisked
- 1 pound cod fillets, cut into medium strips
- 1 ½ cups almond flour
- A pinch of salt and black pepper
- A drizzle of olive oil

Directions:

- In a bowl, mix the flour with salt and pepper and stir.
- Put the eggs in separate bowl.
- Dip fish strips in the eggs and then dredge in flour mix.
- Grease the slow cooker with the olive oil, arrange the coated fish sticks inside, cover, and cook on high for 2 hours.
- Arrange on a platter and serve as an appetizer.

Nutrition:

- Calories - 211
- Fat - 11,9
- Carbs - 2,4
- Protein - 25

LEEK DIP

Serving: 4

Ingredients:

- 4 cups chopped leeks
- 1 cup chicken stock
- ¼ cup olive oil
- A pinch of salt and black pepper
- 4 garlic cloves, minced
- ½ cup lime juice

Directions:

- In your slow cooker, combine all the ingredients, cover and cook on low for 2 hours.
- Blend using an immersion blender, divide into bowls and serve.

Nutrition:

- Calories - 175
- Fat - 13
- Carbs - 15,6
- Protein - 1,8

BEEF LETTUCE WRAPS

Serving: 6

Ingredients:

- 6 lettuce leaves

- 1-pound beef sirloin, chopped
- 1 teaspoon tomato paste
- 5 tablespoons cream cheese
- 1 teaspoon butter
- 1 teaspoon curry powder
- ½ teaspoon paprika

Directions:

- Put chopped beef sirloin in the crockpot.
- Add tomato paste, butter, cream cheese, curry powder, and paprika.
- Mix up the meat mixture and close the crockpot lid.
- Cook beef for 4 hours on High.
- When the beef is cooked, shred it well with the help of the fork.
- Fill the lettuce leaves with the shredded beef and fold them.

Nutrition:

- Calories - 178
- Fat - 8.3
- Carbs - 0.8
- Protein - 23.7

ZINGY BOILED PEANUTS

Serving: 6

Ingredients:

- 1 pound raw peanuts

- 1/3 cup Old Bay seasoning
- ¼ cup kosher salt
- ¼ cup apple cider vinegar
- 1 tbsp. mustard seeds
- 1 bay leaf
- Filtered water, as required

Directions:

- Rinse the peanuts under cold running water and remove any twigs and roots.
- In the bottom of Instant Pot, add all ingredients and enough water to cover the peanuts and stir.
- Place a plate or trivet on top of peanuts.
- Secure the lid and place the pressure valve to "Seal" position.
- Select "MANUAL" and cook under "High Pressure" for about 75-90 minutes.
- Select the "Cancel" and carefully do a "Natural" release.
- Remove the lid and keep aside to cool.
- Drain well and serve.

Nutrition:

- Calories - 4540
- Fat - 37.8g
- Carbs - 0.48g
- Protein - 20g

CHEESECAKE

Serving: 6

Ingredients:

- 3 large eggs, beaten
- 1 cup white sugar
- 3 cups cream cheese, room temperature
- ½ tbsp vanilla extract

Directions:

- Pour the water into the Instant Pot and set a steam rack in the pot.
- In a medium bowl, combine the eggs, sugar, cream cheese, and vanilla.
- Pour the mixture into a baking dish that can fit into the pot.
- Cover the pan tightly with aluminum foil.
- Put the dish on the rack. Secure the lid.
- Select MANUAL and cook at HIGH pressure for 30 minutes.
- When the timer goes off, let the pressure
- Release Naturally
- for 10 minutes, then release any remaining steam manually. Open the lid.
- Let the cheesecake cool for a few minutes and serve.

TENDER ALMOND SHRIMPS

Serving: 4

Ingredients:

- 1 tablespoon almond flakes
- 1 tablespoon almond flour
- 1 oz Parmesan, grated
- ¾ teaspoon cayenne pepper
- 1 tablespoon butter
- ½ cup organic almond milk
- 9 oz shrimps, peeled

Directions:

- Mix up together almond flakes, almond flour, and Parmesan.
- Sprinkle the shrimps with cayenne pepper and place in the crockpot.
- Add almond milk.
- Cook the shrimp for 1.5 hours on High.
- Then open the lid and top the shrimps with Parmesan mixture.
- Close the lid and cook appetizer for 30 minutes on High.

Nutrition:

- Calories - 184
- Fat - 10.7
- Carbs - 3.3
- Protein - 19

CLEAN EATING BLONDIES

Serving: 6

Ingredients:

- ½ can (from a 15 oz can chickpeas, rinsed, drained
- 3 Tbsp pure maple syrup or honey
- ¼ tsp sea salt + extra to garnish
- 1/8 tsp baking soda
- ¼ cup almond butter
- 1 tsp pure vanilla extract
- 1/8 tsp baking powder
- 3 Tbsp baking chocolate chips
- Olive oil, as required

Directions:

- Grease the inside of the slow cooker pot with olive oil. Place a sheet of parchment paper on the bottom as well as slightly on the sides of the slow cooker.
- Add chickpeas, honey, sea salt, baking soda, almond butter, vanilla extract and baking powder into a blender.
- Blend for 30 to 40 seconds or until smooth.
- Pour into the slow cooker. Add half the chocolate chips and fold gently.
- Scatter the remaining chocolate chips on top. Press the chocolate chips lightly into the batter.
- Cover and cook for 2 to 3 hours on low or a toothpick when inserted in the center comes out clean and the edges would be brown.

- Switch off the slow cooker and take out the cooking pot. Place cooking pot on your countertop for 2 hours.
- Carefully remove the blondies along with the parchment paper.
- Cut into 6 equal squares. Sprinkle some sea salt on top and serve.

Nutrition:

- Calories - 150

MINTY GRAPEFRUIT MIX

Serving: 4

Ingredients:

- 1 cup water
- 1 cup maple syrup
- ½ cup chopped minutes
- 2 cups grapefruits, cut into segments

Directions:

- In your slow cooker, combine all the ingredients, cover and cook on low for 2 hours.
- Divide into cups and serve cold.
- Nutrition: 247
- Fat - 0,4
- Carbs - 2,1
- Protein - 1,1

MINI SAUSAGES DELIGHT

Serving: 24

Ingredients:

- 1 pound mini sausages, smoked
- 12 ounces Paleo chili sauce
- 1 cup Paleo grape jelly

Directions:

- Put mini sausages in your slow cooker.
- In a bowl, mix chili sauce with grape jelly and whisk really well.
- Add this to your slow cooker, toss sausages to coat and cook on Low for 4 hours.
- Serve them on a platter.
- Enjoy!

Nutrition:

- Calories - 200
- Fat - 2
- Carbs - 6
- Protein - 12

Printed in Great Britain
by Amazon